D1193820

CLARK COUNTY BOARD OF EDUCATION

From a painting by Forrest W. Orr

This picture shows many things which
you will study about in this book

PATHWAYS · IN · SCIENCE · IV
A COURSE FOR ELEMENTARY SCHOOLS

The Earth and Living Things

By GERALD S. CRAIG

Professor of Natural Sciences
Teachers College, Columbia University

and BEATRICE DAVIS HURLEY

Teacher in Horace Mann School
Teachers College, Columbia University

GINN AND COMPANY

BOSTON · NEW YORK · CHICAGO · LONDON · ATLANTA · DALLAS · COLUMBUS · SAN FRANCISCO

PATHWAYS · IN · SCIENCE
A UNIFIED COURSE FOR ELEMENTARY SCHOOLS

I. We Look About Us
CRAIG AND BURKE

II. Out-of-Doors
CRAIG AND BALDWIN

III. Our Wide, Wide World
CRAIG AND BALDWIN

IV. The Earth and Living Things
CRAIG AND HURLEY

V. Learning About Our World
CRAIG AND CONDRY

VI. Our Earth and Its Story
CRAIG AND JOHNSON

11·43

The Athenæum Press
GINN AND COMPANY · PRO-
PRIETORS · BOSTON · U.S.A.

Preface

There is a widespread movement to recognize the importance of science in the training of children by presenting a program of instruction in science in the schools beginning with the kindergarten and extending through the elementary and secondary schools. Pathways in Science is a series of text books in science designed to meet the demands of this movement by means of introducing a course of carefully graded problems in science for children in Grades I through VI.

The content of this series is the result of an intensive study of elementary science by the authors. These studies[1] involved an analysis of children's interests in science, educated laymen's needs in science, present practices in the elementary school, and an exploration of the various fields of science for challenging themes appropriate to the elementary school.

The "Horace Mann Course of Study"[2] was based upon these studies and was subsequently tried out in a large number of school systems in

[1] Certain Techniques Used in Developing a Course of Study in Science for the Horace Mann Elementary School, Bureau of Publications, Teachers College, Columbia University, New York City, 1927.

[2] Horace Mann Course of Study in Elementary Science, Bureau of Publications, Teachers College, Columbia University, New York City, 1927.

various parts of the country. These try-outs gave
opportunity for widespread criticism and evaluation
of the materials and their grade placement.

"The Earth and Living Things" is organized
about a number of units. These units present a
series of problems which have been found to be
challenging to children and which are designed to
give the child an understanding of certain basic
concepts of the earth on which he lives, the forces
operating to change the surface of the earth, social
life of animals, the interrelation and interdepend-
ence of plants and animals, the economic value of
plants and animals and interpretations of certain
physical phenomena, including gravitation, change
of state, steam and electricity. The book is designed
to help the child orient himself intelligently to the
natural phenomena of his world.

The series definitely conforms to the recommen-
dations and the spirit of the Thirty-first Yearbook,
Part I, of the National Society for the Study of
Education, and the requirements of recent city and
state courses of study in elementary science.

The vocabulary has been checked throughout
by the use of the Buckingham-Dolch Word List.
Whenever over-grade words are needed for the en-
richment of the science vocabulary of the children
they are carefully explained in the text.

Many elementary-school teachers have felt considerable embarrassment in the past because they realized the meagerness of their training in this field. The teacher's manual which accompanies "The Earth and Living Things" is designed to give the teacher an ample background of content in science in a convenient and accessible form. The manual gives a large number of suggested activities, experiments, and procedures which will serve to enrich the classroom instruction. By making use of the manual, which includes a carefully prepared bibliography for teachers, it is possible for classroom teachers to secure considerable training for the teaching of elementary science while conducting the course. Elementary-school teachers need no longer be embarrassed in guiding the child in his interpretation of natural phenomena.

Acknowledgment is made for illustrations on pages 186 and 188, from Linville, Kelly, and Van Cleave's "Textbook in General Zoology" (Ginn and Company); on page 189, from Reinhard's "Witchery of Wasps" (The Century Co.); on page 217, from "In Beaver World," by Enos A. Mills. The authors wish to express their special indebtedness to Dr. B. R. Buckingham for encouragement and guidance that he has given in this undertaking.

G. S. C.
B. D. H.

Contents

Contents

THE EARTH AND LIVING THINGS

The earth is the home of every living thing of which we have any knowledge. It is a great ball spinning through space. Indeed, this ball is so large that, try as hard as they can, it takes flyers at least six days to fly around it.

This earth is full of hundreds of interesting things. If you look up at the top of a volcano, you may see smoke and fire shooting into the air. If you look into the evening sky, you will see stars and planets, some of which are larger than our earth. If you travel through the Grand Canyon, you will see places where the earth is being worn away by wind and water.

Have you ever thought much about the wonders of this world? If you haven't, this book will start you thinking about them. If you have thought about science, these stories will answer some of your questions.

Some of the stories tell of the things other boys and girls about your own age have found out for themselves in their classroom. They have watched bees making honey, ants building tunnels, and spiders spinning webs. They have experimented with dry cells and electric bells and have made electricity work for them.

The pictures were selected to make the book easier for you. They will help you to understand just how the boys and girls did the experiments.

Sometime you may wish to try experiments of your own. You may even find out things which no one ever knew before.

UNIT I

The Earth

Did you ever stop to think what the earth is like?

Have you ever wondered why the earth does not bump into the moon and stars?

Have you ever read what the inside of the earth is like?

Do you know that the earth is really made of solids, liquids, and gases?

You must have many questions to ask about the earth.

You may find the answers to most of your questions by reading the stories about the earth in this book.

Problem 1 · The Earth and Weight

1. The Earth is Our Home

The earth is our home. We live on it. We work and play on the earth. We go from home to school

There are many ways to travel. Can you find four methods of travel shown in this picture?

and back home again. Some of us have traveled a long way by car, train, or boat. It seemed very far as we rode along mile after mile. Yet we stayed upon the earth all the time. We did not leave the earth at all. We can never really leave it.

Did you ever take a trip in an airplane? Did you leave the earth in it? Some of you think that of course you left the earth when you took your airplane ride. But you really did not. You left only one part of it. You left the solid part of the earth. You flew into the air. The air is really part of the earth, too. The air which you breathe is made up of gases. We say that it is the gaseous part of the earth.

If you rode in a hydroplane, you took off from, and landed on, the water. You might think that you had surely left the earth then. But you didn't. Water is also part of the earth. It is the liquid part. Can you see now that you really never left the earth at all when you took your airplane ride? You only left the solid part of it and flew into the gaseous part of it, the air.

Here is something which may seem strange. We can fly into the air. We can throw things into the air. We can watch birds fly in the air. We can fly our kites when the wind is strong. But none of these things can stay in the air forever. They all come down to the solid part of the earth.

Birds fly long distances. They fly miles and miles sometimes. They cannot keep right on

This aviator was forced to leave his plane. By using the huge parachute he landed safely

flying all the time, however. When they stop flying they come to the land part of the earth to rest.

Aviators know that they must take along a supply of gasoline in order to stay up in the air. If the gasoline supply runs out, the motor won't run.

If the motor stops running, the plane will crash to the solid part of the earth. When an aviator is forced to leave his plane he uses a parachute so that he will not fall too fast. But even the parachute cannot keep the pilot from falling to the solid part of the earth.

Did you ever try to throw a ball so high into the air that it would not come down? Could you do it? No matter how hard you tried to throw the ball it would always come back down. Even the biggest and strongest giant you ever read about could not throw far enough to do that. The ball would come back.

All things which fly into the air come back again to the solid part of the earth. Should you like to know why?

2. The Pull of the Earth

What a queer world this would be

If apples fell from the tree up into the air instead of down to the ground.

If your ball would never come back to earth after you had thrown it into the air.

If you could jump over a house as easily as you can jump over a fence.

If you could float around in the air just as a bird flies through the sky.

If you could fall from a high window to the ground and not hurt yourself.

If water should spill up toward the ceiling instead of down toward the floor.

Did you ever stop to think why things like these do not happen? They never have happened, and they probably never will. Ever since the world began things have been falling down instead of up. This is the reason why.

The earth pulls all kinds of things to it. It pulls everything about it. This power the earth has of pulling everything to it is called *gravity*.

No one really knows just what gravity is. Scientists are people who have studied about the earth and the stars and living things. They know how gravity works. They know that it is the force which brings a ball down when it is thrown into the air. They know that it is the force which brings rain, snow, and hail down from the clouds. They know that it is the force which makes an apple fall down instead of up when it leaves the tree. They know that gravity holds cars and houses to the earth.

In fact, gravity is the force which keeps the

c

water from spilling out of oceans. It keeps the
air from leaving the earth. It holds the soil and
rocks to the earth. It holds the earth together.
Everything on the earth and about the earth is
pulled toward the solid part of the earth.

You have already been told that the pull of
the earth's gravity keeps the air, or atmosphere,
near land. All other bodies in the sky also have
a force called gravitation which holds atmospheres,
or gases, to them. The sun has more gases than the
earth because it is so much heavier. The atmosphere, or gases, of the sun is entirely different from
that of the earth. The heavier the body the more
pull it has. The moon is too small to hold much
atmosphere. The earth and the sun have probably pulled the moon's atmosphere away from it.
Can people live where there is no air? Do you
believe that people live on the moon?

3. Why Some Things Weigh More than Others

Things which can be seen or touched are sometimes called objects. Gravity gives objects weight.
How much do you weigh? Did you ever stop to
think why you weigh what you do? It is gravity

This boy is finding out how much gravity is
pulling down upon his body. Gravity gives
him his weight. It gives all objects their weight

which makes you weigh what you do. If the scales
say that you weigh fifty-nine pounds it means that
gravity is pulling down upon your body with a

pull equal to fifty-nine pounds. Suppose you weigh sixty-seven pounds. The pull of gravity upon your body is sixty-seven pounds. We mean by weight the pull of gravity.

All things do not weigh the same. You are not so heavy as your father because gravity does not pull so hard upon you as it does upon your father.

4. Why Some Objects Float and Other Objects Sink

It may be fun to find out why some objects float upon water and other objects sink to the bottom. First let us experiment with a few objects to see what will float and what will sink.

Fill a large pan or a pail with water. Collect some objects which you would like to test, or try out, in the water. Below is a list of objects that some children put into their pan of water:

corks
small blocks of wood
nails

small stones
2 small tin boxes
a sponge

lumps of sugar

celluloid toys ⎰ fish
⎱ turtle
frog

a penny
steel magnets

Why do some of these objects float and
others sink? Which ones will sink?

They had fun dropping them into the pan and
watching some float and others sink. The blocks
of wood and the corks stayed on top of the water.
The toy fish and frog and turtle also floated. The
empty tin boxes floated, too. These objects are
all lighter for their size than water. That is why
they stayed on top of it.

The children tried pushing these light objects
down to the bottom of the pan. Every time they

The top and cork float because they
are lighter for their size than water

let go of the cork or fish or block, up it came to
the surface again. The children were puzzled.

Let us see just what made these things float.
We have said that they floated because they were
lighter for their size than the water.

Gravity made the toys push down upon the

water. When they pushed down upon the water, the water pushed back upon them. Because the water was heavier, it would not let the objects push it out of their way. There was nothing else for them to do but to float.

Another way to say the same thing is that the water pressed on the cork and the toys harder than they could press down on the water; so they had to rise to the top.

Let us see what happened when the children dropped some of the other objects into the pan. They dropped a stone into the water, and it went to the bottom. The steel magnets also sank. The nails and the penny did the same thing.

All of these objects are heavier for their size than water. They pushed *down* on the water harder than the water pushed *up* on them, and so they pushed some of the water out of their way and sank.

The lumps of sugar did something different. They started sinking and got smaller and smaller as they went down until they could not be seen any more. They dissolved and became a part of the water.

Next came the sponge. What do you think it did? For a little while it floated. Then it slowly sank. Let us see why it didn't go down right away. A sponge has many holes in it. These holes are full of air. When the sponge was put on the water, the water pushed the air out of the holes and stayed in the holes itself. Each time a hole was filled with water the sponge got heavier than it had been when the hole was filled with air. That is why the sponge sank slowly to the bottom.

Now the children played with the tin boxes. They put them both on the water. Both of them floated. Then the children had some fun. They put a couple of stones into one can and crushed in the sides of the can. When they put it back on the water it sank at once. The children had now made the can heavier for its size than water.

Have you ever wondered why a great steel ship floats upon the ocean? Steel is heavier than water. Why doesn't it sink to the bottom?

The ship is just like the tin box. It is lighter for its size than the water it pushes out of its way.

If the ship were a solid block of steel it would sink just as the nails and the magnets sank.

Did you ever see a heavily loaded ship? The water comes a good way up the sides of the ship. Then have you seen the same boat when it was empty? It was farther out of the water than be-

Can you tell why one of these boats is floating farther out of the water than the other?

fore. The heavy load had been taken ashore. Now
the boat was not as heavy for its size as it had
been before. The change made the ship float
farther out of the water.

5. What is *Up* and What is *Down*?

We have been saying that things always fall
down. We have said that gravity pulls objects
down. Do you know just what *down* means? Do
you know just what *up* means?

Suppose you should ask John, a North Ameri-

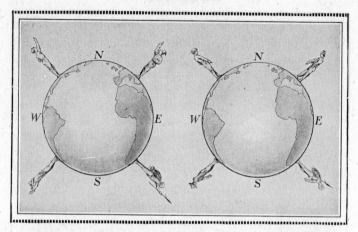

In the picture on the left the boys are pointing
up. In the picture on the right the boys are pointing *down*. Up is away from the center of the
earth and down is toward the center of the earth

can boy, to point *up*. Which way would he point?
Suppose you should ask Lopez, a South American
child, to point *up*. Which way would he point? Suppose you should ask Ming, a Chinese boy, to point
up. Which way would he point? Or ask Abdul, an
Egyptian boy, to point *up*. Which way would he
point? Would they all point the same way for *up*?

Above is a picture which shows the direction in
which each would point. Each child is pointing
into the sky for *up*. None are pointing in the same
direction. *Up* is always away from the center of
the earth.

Now, suppose you should ask John, Lopez, Ming, and Abdul to point down. Which way would they point? Would they point the way the children in the picture are pointing? Down is toward the center of the earth. It is the direction in which objects always fall.

 Things to Think About

1. Suppose that gravity should stop working for a day. What might happen to the air, the clouds, houses, people, and the sea?

2. Why does a solid piece of steel sink when put in water, while a steel boat floats in water?

3. What makes some objects lighter than other objects? Why is a feather lighter than a piece of lead?

4. What is the force that makes all things fall toward the center of the earth?

5. Gravity is a very important force. It holds atmosphere to the earth. If this force were not present there would be no life upon the earth. Animals and plants need air in order to live. Boys and girls need oxygen, one of the gases of the air, to make them strong and healthy. Many men who have studied about the moon think that it has no atmosphere at all. If this is true, could there be any life, as we know it, on the moon?

 **The Earth**

Things to Do

1. Take a stone in one hand and an eraser in the other. Stand on a chair. Drop them both at the same time. Which one reaches the floor first? Why did they fall down?

2. Toss a stone and a rubber ball into the air the same distance. Which one reaches the earth first?

3. Ask your teacher to read to you about how a scientist named Galileo taught people about gravity.

4. Weigh yourself. From a table of weights find out whether you weigh enough for your height and age. If you do not, try to gain weight by following these health rules:

> *a.* Eat plenty of cereals, fresh fruits, and green leafy vegetables.
> *b.* Drink at least six glasses of water and four glasses of milk daily.
> *c.* Play outdoors at least four hours a day.
> *d.* Sleep eleven hours each night in a well-ventilated room.
> *e.* Rest for a few minutes after each meal.
> *f.* Take a bath at least twice a week.
> *g.* Brush your teeth at least twice a day to keep them clean.

Problem 2 · What the Earth is Like

1. The Solid Part of the Earth

The earth has three parts. We know most about the solid part of our earth. We call it the land part. It is the part upon which we live. We build our houses, churches, schools, and stores upon it. We spend most of our lives upon it. It is our home. Sometimes we take an airplane ride and leave the land. Sometimes we take a long boat trip upon the water. But we always return to the land part of the earth. We make our homes on the land part.

So far as we can tell, men have probably always lived on the land. For a long time men were afraid to go to sea because they thought strange animals, such as serpents and monsters, waited to capture them. Columbus was one of the first men who dared to get very far from land. Even his sailors wanted to turn back because they were afraid.

It has not been a very long time since men began to leave the land to fly in the air. Both sailors and aviators come back to the land, for this is their home.

The land, or solid, part of the earth is very

Here is a picture of one of the Wright brothers in their glider at Kittyhawk, North Carolina. This glider was one of the first heavier-than-air craft ever flown successfully

important in our living. It is here that we raise food to eat. We could not live without food. Plants grow where there is soil. We either eat some of these plants for food or animals eat them. Then we eat the animals.

We live at the surface of the earth. The air goes only a short distance above the surface. We cannot fly far above the earth's surface. The highest distance man has flown into the air is about ten miles.

Professor Augustus Piccard's balloon, in which
he and his assistant were able to reach the
height of ten miles into the atmosphere. No
one before had ever reached such a height

Recently a famous scientist, Dr. Piccard, rose
to a height of ten miles. He designed a balloon
with a metal air-tight basket in which he and his
assistant rode. They used oxygen tanks, just as
aviators do, to give them a supply of oxygen. Other
flyers are experimenting in the same way. Some
have gone higher than ten miles. The mines which
are dug below the earth's surface are not over a
mile deep. So you see we live right at the surface.
You remember that it is four thousand miles to the

center of the earth. When you think of this great distance, you will see that we can go only a very little way up into the air or down into mines.

Draw a circle on the blackboard to stand for, or represent, the earth. Draw a line from the center of the circle to the outside. Your line is short, but a line from the center of the real earth to the outside would be four thousand miles long. Call the line you just drew four thousand miles long.

Now make a dot on the line which would show how deep the deepest mine is.

Would it be near the center of the circle?

Next draw a circle around the earth which would show the path of an airplane which is flying about eight miles high around the earth.

2. The Inside of the Earth

Have you ever wondered just what the inside of the earth is like? Has anyone ever been down to see what it is like? No; no one has ever been down into the earth farther than the deepest mine. This is only a step compared with the depth of the earth.

Many queer stories have been told about what was under the earth's surface. Men for a long time thought that there must be a huge furnace inside

Many persons, seeing a volcano sending out smoke, came to believe that the earth had a crust somewhat like the crust of a pie. Is this true?

the earth. You can easily see how they happened to believe that. There are mountains in some parts of the earth which send forth melted rock. They are called volcanoes. There are springs, called geysers, which throw hot water and steam out of the ground. Men saw this hot rock and steam shooting from inside the earth. What else could there be but a great furnace which could melt rock and boil water?

For a long time most people feared that the top, or crust, of the earth would burst and that hot melted rock would pour out and destroy their homes. In fact, that very thing has happened in many places. People thought that all of the inside of the earth was hot. They thought only the top, or crust, part was cool and solid. They thought this pie-crust top was only a few miles thick. You can see how afraid they must have been. Think how you would feel if you thought your home would be destroyed any minute.

Scientists differ in their opinions as to just what the inside of the earth is like. Some believe that it is a molten mass. Others believe that it is a solid mass. Many think that the inside of the earth is made up of two metals, nickel and iron. All scientists do agree, however, that this mass inside the earth is rigid, or firm, and that there is no danger of the earth's caving in, as some persons used to believe.

3. The Water Part of the Earth

Another part of the earth is made up of water. The largest bodies of water are the great oceans, the Atlantic, Pacific, Indian, and Arctic. All the lakes, rivers, and smaller streams help to make up the liquid, or water, part of the earth.

Do you know that this liquid part of our earth is very important? Look at your globe. Can you

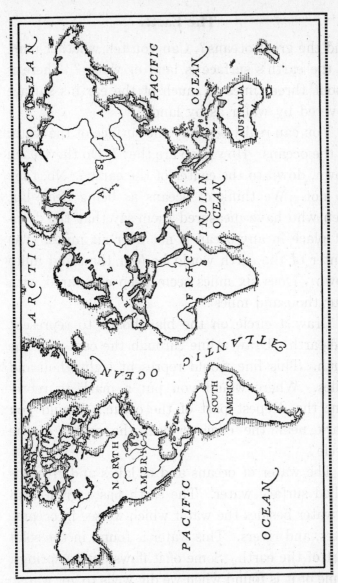

Find the large bodies of water on this map

find the great oceans? Can you tell whether more
of the earth's surface is land or water? There is
about three times as much of the earth's surface
covered by water as by land.

You can really see only the surface of the water
of the oceans. How deep are they? Do they reach
down, down to the center of the earth? No, they
do not. We think of oceans as being deep, but
men who have measured them say that the deepest place in any ocean is not over six miles. The
center of the earth would be four thousand miles
down. Does six miles seem deep compared with
four thousand miles?

Draw a circle on the blackboard to represent
the earth. Draw a line through the center of the
earth. This line would represent eight thousand
miles. Where would you put a mark to represent the deepest part of the ocean? Would you
mark near the edge or near the center of the
circle?

The water of oceans and of lakes and rivers is
called surface water. The earth has a great deal
of water besides the water which we see in oceans,
lakes, and rivers. This water is found in the solid
part of the earth. Some of it flows out as springs.
Some of it is found when we dig wells to get water.

Water found in the solid part of the earth is called ground water. Both surface and ground water are purified and used for drinking. Water has many other uses which we shall learn about later.

4. The Part of the Earth Made Up of Air and Gases

Some people think that the hard, or solid, part of the earth is the outer part of the earth. This is not really true. You have already learned that the air which we breathe is a part of the earth. It is made of gases. We cannot see these gases, but we can breathe them. One of these gases, called oxygen, keeps us alive. The part of the earth which is made up of gases we call the atmosphere.

We live at the bottom of this ocean of air. We know that gravity holds us to the solid part of the earth. Gravity also pulls this ocean of air toward the solid part of the earth. We have learned that this ocean of air is called the atmosphere. The atmosphere is made up of gases which you cannot see.

Many people think that the air is everywhere. They think it goes on and on out into the sky. This is not true. The atmosphere forms a blanket which goes clear around the earth, but it does not go up into space very far. This blanket of atmosphere is thicker and heavier down close to the ground. We say the air is denser near the earth.

As one travels up into the atmosphere the air gets thinner and thinner. Did you ever climb a very high mountain? The atmosphere at the top is thinner than it is at the bottom. You will notice that it is harder for you to breathe on a mountain top than it is at the foot of the mountain. Now we say the air is less dense, or thinner, than it was at the foot of the mountain.

One of the highest mountains in the world is Mt. Everest. It is about five and one-half miles high. No one has yet reached its top.

Aviators have never been able to fly more than eight miles up into the atmosphere. The air is very thin so high up as that. That means there is less oxygen, and oxygen is a gas in the air that we must breathe in order to live. Men who fly high wear oxygen helmets to supply them with more oxygen for breathing.

The atmosphere goes up farther than eight miles. Scientists have tried to find out just how far up the atmosphere does go. Many of them think that there is still some atmosphere even

Mount Everest viewed from Birch Hill at twilight. This is the highest mountain in the world. Notice that the peaks are covered with snow

more than one hundred miles from the ground. No one could live in the atmosphere at that distance from the ground because there would not be enough air for breathing. Most of the earth's atmosphere is close to the solid part of the earth. It makes a blanket which goes clear around the earth's surface.

Now you can see why we say that we live at the bottom of an ocean of air. Over our heads there is air for one hundred miles or more. It is

The peel of an apple is something like the earth's atmosphere

over America. It is over boys and girls in Holland, China, Africa, and every other country. These boys and girls are a little like fish in a lake. Fish are surrounded by water. Boys and girls are surrounded by air.

Here is something which may help you to understand better about the earth's atmosphere. You have all peeled an apple. The peel of the apple is a little like the atmosphere of the earth. The peel is the outer covering which goes all around the apple. The atmosphere is the outer covering which goes all around the solid part of the earth.

Have you ever stopped to think how thick through our earth is? We know that the center of the earth is four thousand miles from the surface. If you started digging through the earth you would have to dig eight thousand miles before you would come to the other side. Could you ever really do that? No one has ever dug very far into the earth.

Make a circle on the blackboard to represent the solid part of the earth. Draw a line through the center of it. This line represents eight thousand miles, because the earth is eight thousand miles through. With a piece of colored chalk shade in the atmosphere which goes clear around the earth's surface. How much shall you shade? Remember that most scientists think that the atmosphere goes one hundred miles or more above the earth.

5. Clouds in the Atmosphere

The clouds that we see in the sky are in the earth's atmosphere. If you have climbed high mountains you have probably passed through

Clouds often come very near the earth. The
clouds in this picture are below the mountain tops

clouds to get to the top. If you have had many
airplane rides you must surely have passed through
clouds. If you have ever been in a fog you have
been in a cloud. Fogs are clouds which have come
very close to the ground.

Clouds often look as though they were nearer
the moon than the earth, but they are not. The
moon is two hundred and fifty thousand miles
away from the earth. Most clouds are within one
or two miles of the land part of the earth.

Things to Think About

1. Why don't scientists know more about the inside of the earth than they do?

2. As scientists work they often discover new truths which show that old ideas are false. Can you think of any things which people used to think were true that we now know are false?

3. Clouds often come very near the ground. Why do they sometimes do this?

Things to Do

Can you put the right word in the blank in each sentence below? Do not write in the book.

1. The earth has _ _ _ _ _ parts.

2. The land part of the earth gives us our _ _ _ _ _.

3. Man has flown only about _ _ _ _ _ miles into the air.

4. Men have dug only about _ _ _ _ _ mile down into the earth.

5. There is _ _ _ _ _ times as much water as land on the earth's surface.

6. The earth's blanket is the _ _ _ _ _.

7. The ocean of air is about _ _ _ _ _ miles deep.

8. _ _ _ _ _ holds the air to the land.

9. Clouds are in the _ _ _ _ _ part of the earth.

Problem 3 · Solids, Liquids, and Gases

1. Changing Solids, Liquids, and Gases

Betty and Jack had heard about important people called scientists. They knew that scientists could change the color, size, and form, or shape, of many things by working with them. They knew that scientists had discovered many things about the earth which might not have been known if it had not been for their studying about them.

Jack and Betty wanted to do some experimenting. They decided to ask Miss Bell, their teacher, to help them.

"Oh, Miss Bell," said Betty and Jack in one breath as they both pushed through the door of the schoolhouse, "we have the best idea for something to do. Will you help us?"

Miss Bell knew the children. She knew that they had had their heads together again. When Jack and Betty got to thinking, something was always sure to come of it.

Betty started to explain that they had decided to play they were scientists. Jack couldn't wait for his turn. He interrupted, "You see, Miss Bell, we have been reading about the parts of the earth. Isn't there some experiment we can do to learn more about them?"

Miss Bell needed no more time for thinking. "Do you know that sometimes the solid part of the earth changes to liquid and that the liquid part of the earth changes to gas?"

"No, how?" asked several other of Miss Bell's children, all of them much interested.

A table was cleared quickly. A couple of pans were brought from a cupboard. Miss Bell brought some canned heat and some matches. Now what was about to happen?

Miss Bell said, "I should like a solid for this experiment."

One child brought a pencil. Another a ribbon, another a book, and still another a piece of chalk.

"I'm not going to use any of these things. They are all solids, but I want to start with another solid, if I may. Jack, will you run outside and bring in one of the big icicles which are hanging on the window?"

The children looked puzzled. Jack soon came back with the icicle.

By heating icicles these children
are changing a solid to a liquid

"Where shall I put it? It's cold," he shouted.

"Put it in this pan," Betty suggested. "What
are you going to do with this solid?"

"How do you think this solid can be changed?"
asked Miss Bell.

A child near the table noticed that the ice was
changing already. "I know," he shouted. "Heat
it!"

No sooner said than done. The canned heat
was lighted and placed under the pan of ice. The
children watched eagerly. Slowly the ice disap-
peared. It melted to water.

"But, Miss Bell," asked John, "the solid icicle changed its form and is now water. What made it do so?"

"Can any one answer John's question?" asked Miss Bell.

Some one said that ice melted when it got warm.

"How warm?" asked Miss Bell.

No one knew. So she told them that when the temperature gets to be 32° Fahrenheit ice turns to water. "If the temperature goes below 32° Fahrenheit, then the water freezes into ice," added Miss Bell. "That is why your father, if he drives a car, has to watch the thermometer in the winter. He has to be sure that the water in the car radiator doesn't freeze. Do you know what would happen if it did freeze?"

"Yes," answered Jack. "Once my father forgot to put alcohol in the radiator of our car, and the water froze to ice and burst the radiator."

"What does Fahrenheit mean?" asked John.

"Fahrenheit is the name of the scientist who made one of the thermometers which we use a great deal," answered Miss Bell.

Betty interrupted to ask, "But, Miss Bell, you can't change water into anything but ice, can you?"

Can you see steam?

"That's just what I was about to show you," said Miss Bell. "Let's heat some water and see what happens."

Miss Bell boiled some water in a teakettle. She asked the children to point to the steam. Mary pointed to the small cloud that seemed to come from the kettle.

"No," said Miss Bell, "that is not steam. You can not see steam."

"Oh," said John, "the steam is next to the spout where you can't see anything."

By heating solid iron very hot it turns to liquid

John was right. Steam is invisible, that is, it cannot be seen. The cloud was made up of water, where the steam, or gaseous part, had changed back into water. Watch water boiling. The steam will be just above the water.

The children were eager to know more about changing solids to liquids and liquids to gases. Miss Bell told them that when solid iron was heated very hot it melted and turned to liquid.

Every child in Miss Bell's room was glad Jack

c

and Betty had got their heads together. They had enjoyed doing experiments so much that they wanted to do other things at school which would help them to understand things better. Miss Bell told them that on another day she would tell them more about the differences between solids, liquids, and gases.

2. Differences between Solids, Liquids, Gases

A few days later Miss Bell went on with the work about solids, liquids, and gases. The children wanted to know how these three things were different.

"Is your desk a liquid?" asked Miss Bell. The children laughed. They knew that their desks were solids. Miss Bell wanted to know how they knew desks were solids.

"Because they keep their shapes," Alice said.

"Because they are hard," added Betty.

"Because they stay where they are put," said Jack.

"Alice is right," said Miss Bell. "Solids do keep their shape. They do not flow around. Did you ever see a desk go flowing around the room? But Betty is not right. Jelly is a solid. Blankets are solids, but they are all soft. Jack, your answer was right. Solids do stay where they are put. They do not flow about."

"What about liquids?" asked Jack.

"I know," said Betty. "Solids keep their shape. Liquids don't. They flow about."

"Liquids have no shape of their own," said Miss Bell. "The sea water takes the shape of the bottom of the ocean. The water in a pail takes the shape of the pail. Liquids take the shape of the pan, pond, lake, ocean, or whatever else they are in."

"What about gases?" asked Betty. "How are they different?"

"We live in an atmosphere made up of gases," said Miss Bell. "These gases we breathe are called air. Does air flow about, or does it keep its shape?"

"Air flows about," said Betty.

"That's right," answered Miss Bell. "But gases spread out more than liquids. They try to fill all the space there is. Gases stay near the earth because of gravity's pull. The air would probably wander away from the earth if gravity were not strong enough to hold it."

Miss Bell wrote the following questions on the

board for the children to answer. Betty and Jack
answered all of them.

See how many you can answer.

1. Could you walk *on* water?
2. Could you walk around *in* a solid?
3. Could you walk *through* the air?
4. Could you sit down *on* water?
5. Does a solid keep its shape?
6. Does a liquid keep its shape?
7. How is a solid different from a liquid?
8. How is a liquid different from a gas?

3. What Happens When Water Freezes

Another day the children in Miss Bell's room
were doing an experiment. They wanted to see
what happens when water freezes. They filled a
glass jar full of water right up to the very top.
Then they screwed the cover on tightly and set
the jar in a snow bank where it would be cold.

They came to school early the next morning.
They found the water frozen and the jar broken.
Miss Bell told them that when water turns to a
solid it needs more room than when it is a liquid.
There was no more room in the jar, so the ice had
to break it to make room for itself.

This jar broke because the ice which formed inside did not have enough room

These rocks have been cracked by the water freezing under them

"Now I see why dad's radiator burst when the water froze in it," said John. "The ice needed more room, so it burst the pipes."

"Have you ever seen cracks and bumps in the sidewalks in the spring of the year?" asked Miss Bell. "These were made because the water under the sidewalks froze and needed more room. It cracked the sidewalks, or made them hump up.

"The same thing happens in rocks. Water runs under them, between them, and into their cracks. When it gets cold this water freezes. When water freezes it expands or spreads out. The rocks have to break to make room for the ice."

 Things to Think About

1. Sometimes in the winter you will find that the milk in the bottle on the porch has frozen and has pushed the cap and the cream above the top of the bottle. Why?

2. Why is steam invisible?

3. What three forms is water able to take? What makes it change from one to another?

4. What would happen if water froze at 60° Fahrenheit?

5. When you go camping you must be careful to drink good water. Water sometimes carries tiny plants called bacteria, some of which give persons diseases of different kinds. Even though the water looks good it may contain

harmful bacteria, which you cannot see. If you are camping in a new place, be sure you carry enough water with you to last until you can inquire about a good source of pure water. In case you cannot find out about the water, you had better play safe by boiling the water you use for drinking. What does boiling the water do to the harmful bacteria in it?

 *Things to Do*

1. See how many things you can add to the list below.

Solids	Liquids	Gases
ice	water	steam
cloth	milk	oxygen

2. Put some water from the faucet into one pan. Put some water with alcohol in it into another pan. Place them on the window sill. Hang a thermometer on the window. See how cold it is when the liquid in each pan freezes. Which freezes first?

3. Here is something for you to try. It will help you to understand why woolen clothing is better for cold winter days than for hot summer ones.

Place a piece of woolen cloth over a patch of snow and beside it place a piece of cotton cloth. Remove the two pieces of cloth after a short time and see which patch has the most snow left under it.

Now answer these questions:

    a. Under which cloth did the snow melt faster?

    b. What caused it to melt faster under one cloth than under the other cloth?

UNIT II
The Changing Earth

The earth has not always looked the same as it does now. It is millions of years since the earth was young. During all these years many interesting things have happened to change the appearance of the great spinning ball which keeps on turning about the sun. High mountains have risen out of the valleys. Small islands have been swallowed up entirely by the sea. Smoking volcanoes have shot hot melted rock into the air, and terrible earthquakes have cracked the earth's crust. You may want to know just how and why such queer things have happened to the earth. The next chapters will tell you about them.

Problem 1 · How the Earth Moves

1. The Earth is a Spinning Ball

If we could leave the earth and go traveling around among the objects in the sky, what strange things we should see! There would be stars which are so hot that anything within thousands of miles of them would melt.

Some objects in the sky are cold and uncomfortable. The moon is like that. It is so cold on the moon at times that scientists believe no plants or animals can live upon it. Plants and animals, including people, need both heat and light in order to live.

Why couldn't we take such a trip? Gravity wouldn't let us, would it? We could not get far enough out into the sky to look back. But if we could, what should we see?

The earth is a great, round ball. It keeps whirling around all the time. You have often played at spinning a top. The earth is spinning around just as a top spins. The top soon stops spinning and needs to be spun again. Our earth is not like that. It never stops going around. It started turning a long, long time ago and has been

The earth and the top both spin around

spinning ever since. Do you know what we say the earth is doing when it is spinning around? We say that the earth is *rotating*. It means that the earth is turning round and round.

The top which you play with rotates many times in a minute. It whirls very fast. The earth rotates fast, too. But it is so very large that it takes it twenty-four hours to turn completely around once. Just think how large it is! You would have to travel twenty-five thousand miles to get around it once.

The candle represents the sun. It can light only half of the earth at one time

You have learned that the earth is round. As it rotates, only half of it is turned toward the sun at a time. Since the sun gives the earth its heat and light, only half of it is heated and lighted at one time. While the half which is facing the sun is having day, the other half, which is not facing it, is having night.

Here is something to do to help you understand the earth's rotation better. Follow these directions carefully. Place a globe on the table or the floor. Place a lighted candle several feet from the globe to represent the sun. Find the place where

The hands of the clock move to the
right. The earth rotates to the left

you live. Now turn the globe so that the lighted
candle, which represents the sun, comes up in the
east and sets in the west for your town. Keep
on rotating the globe. Be sure that you are rotating it in the opposite way from the way the
hands of a clock move. The picture above will
show you how to rotate the globe.

Notice as you rotate the globe that the light
from the candle, which represents the sun, falls
only on the half of the globe which is facing it.
This half is having day. The half of the globe
which is turned away from the candle sun is not
receiving light and is having night.

When it is morning where we live our half of
the earth is just turning toward the sun. Then

we get heat and light from the sun. By night our half has rotated so far that it is turning away from the sun. Then we no longer receive heat and light from the sun.

Once each day the Chinese, who are opposite us, are turned toward the sun. Later, as the earth rotates, Russia faces the sun and it has day. A few hours later England has light because England is turned toward the sun. The light starts across the Atlantic Ocean. When it reaches America, we start to get up. When we are getting up, the Chinese boys and girls are just going to bed. Do you know why?

2. The Earth is Turning around the Sun

While the earth is rotating it is also moving around the sun. It rotates, or spins itself around, once every twenty-four hours. It takes the earth three hundred and sixty-five and one-quarter days to move once around the sun. This movement around the sun is called revolution. We say that the earth revolves around the sun.

You may wonder why the earth does not fall into the sun. There is a reason why this doesn't happen. The movement of the earth keeps the earth going in its path year after year. The earth revolves in a path around the sun. It does not stop moving because there is nothing to stop it.

While the earth revolves once around the sun, it rotates three hundred and sixty-five and one-quarter times.

Do you remember that the rotation of the earth causes day and night? The revolution of the earth marks a period of time, too. The three hundred and sixty-five and one-quarter days that it takes the earth to revolve once around the sun make one year. When you were two years old how many times had the earth revolved about the sun since you were born? When you are fifteen years old, how many trips will the earth have taken around the sun?

While the earth revolves around the sun, another body in the sky revolves around *it*. The moon revolves around the earth. It takes about thirty days for the moon to revolve once around the earth. Every time that the moon goes around the earth once almost a month has passed.

Indians used to measure time by moons. Our month is almost the same as their moon. In old Indian legends you will often see a sentence like this, "He was nine moons old." How old would nine moons be?

Things to Think About

1. What makes day and night?

2. Why don't we get as much light from the moon at night as we get from the sun during the day?

3. Some one has said that the earth makes him think of a giant roast of meat rotating before a great fire. Can you see why?

4. Why is half of the earth always dark?

5. Why do one day and one night together last twenty-four hours?

6. The longest distance around the earth is about twenty-five thousand miles at the equator, and the earth turns around every twenty-four hours. About how many miles does the earth go every hour? Is that faster than a fast train goes?

7. As you look at the earth, you would not believe that you were going so fast. There is no jar or shaking as there is on a train. Can you tell why?

8. Scientists tell us that people who live in a temperate climate live longer than those who live in very hot or very cold climates. Eskimos of the far north and natives of the tropical jungle lands have shorter lives than people who live in milder climates. Many plants grow better in temperate regions, too. Of course, this means there is more of the food of the world grown in the temperate parts of the earth. Can you work better when the day is neither too hot nor too cold? What temperature is best for us to live and work in?

c

 *Things to Do*

1. Find two countries on your globe that are exactly opposite each other. Revolve the globe around a play sun. When one country is having day what is the other country having? Why?

2. It is a good thing that we have both days and nights. What would happen if we had daylight all of the time?

3. It would be fun to find out how we happen to have the calendar we now use. Find out about the ancient Egyptian calendar. It was not like ours. Some persons want to change our calendar so that there would be thirteen months of twenty-eight days each with one extra day known as New Year's Day. Every four years there would be another extra day called Leap Year Day. These two days would not appear on the calendar.

Problem 2 · How Old is the Earth?

1. The Earth is Old

Jack and Betty had another question which they wanted answered. It was, "How old is the earth, anyway?"

Jack said, "It must have been born before father was."

Betty laughed, "Of course it was, years and years before. Why, it was even born before our great-grandfathers lived."

"Well, I guess it was," said John. "It is older than Columbus. You remember that he came to America in 1492. The world had to be made before he could sail the ocean."

"How long ago is 1492?" asked Miss Bell. They figured out that it was more than four hundred years ago that Columbus sailed to America.

"That's a long time," said Betty.

"But that is only a minute compared with the earth's real age," said Miss Bell. "The earth has had millions of birthdays. No one knows exactly how many. But just think of being millions of years old!"

"The earth is older than any of the people that

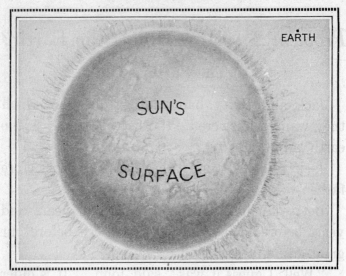

EARTH

SUN'S

SURFACE

The size of the sun compared with the size of the earth

have ever lived upon it. Even the earliest Indians, Egyptians, and Hebrews were not so old
as the earth. It is older than its mountains, lakes,
and valleys. It is millions of years old."

"Is there anything older than the earth?"
asked Betty.

"Nothing on the earth is older than the earth,"
said Miss Bell. "But there are things in the sky
which are older than the earth."

"Is the sun older?" asked Jack.

"Yes," said Miss Bell, "the sun and the stars
are much older than the earth."

© Field Museum of Natural History

The earth was young long, long ago.
It had no plants or animals then

2. The Earth Has Changed Its Looks Many Times

When the children found out that the earth really was very, very old, they became more curious than ever about it. "Has it always looked as it does now?" they asked Miss Bell.

"Oh, my, no," said Miss Bell. "The earth has changed its looks many times. If we could go to a movie called 'The Story of the Earth,' what an interesting one it would be. In fact, the earth has changed so much that if we could see it as it looked millions of years ago we should hardly know it."

"Just how did it look as long ago as that?" asked Betty.

"Scientists tell us that it was covered with hard rock when it was young," said Miss Bell.

"What made it change from hard rock?" asked Jack.

"That is a long story," said Miss Bell. "Should you like to have me tell you about it?"

"Please do," the children answered all together.

3. How the Earth Got Its Atmosphere

"At first the solid part of the earth was made up entirely of rock," began Miss Bell. "After a while the earth started to collect an atmosphere. Volcanoes helped to give the earth its atmosphere. When they poured out melted rock, they also sent out smoke and gases. These gases became part of the earth's atmosphere. You see, gravity held the gases near the earth.

"These gases moved about as they do today, forming what we call wind. Wind has done much to change the looks of the earth. It has kept blowing against the solid rocks and wearing little bits off. These little bits have been blown here, there, and everywhere. Year after year the little bits of rock kept hitting other rocks and wearing them off, too. All of these little bits of rock formed soil."

4. How the Earth Got Its Water

"How did there happen to be water?" asked Betty.

"I was just going to tell you about water," said Miss Bell. "Water has played an important part in changing the earth, too. One of the gases in the atmosphere was water vapor. After a while the atmosphere could not hold any more water vapor. Then the earth had its first rain. Ever since, when there is too much water for the atmosphere to hold, the pull of gravity causes it to fall as rain, snow, sleet, or hail.

"This water which fell kept hitting the solid rock. Years and years passed. Water still kept hitting the solid rocks and wearing off the corners a little."

"Have you ever gathered stones from a stream? Many of the stones in the stream have no sharp

Rushing water wears away the rocks

corners on them. This is because the water has worn the corners down, making the stones smooth."

"How can water do that?" interrupted Jack.

"The water in the brooks, rivers, and oceans moves little bits of sand, rocks, and pebbles about. They rub against one another and rub little bits off from one another. This takes a long, long time. It has been going on ever since the first water fell upon the earth. It is still going on, but so slowly that we hardly notice it."

Things to Think About

1. How long do most people live? How long is a hundred years? Think how many hundreds of years it takes to make a million. Is the earth over a million years old?

2. How did the earth get its atmosphere?

3. Why does it sometimes rain and sometimes snow?

4. What animals lived on the earth when it was young?

5. Which is older — the sun or the earth?

6. The earth is not the oldest thing we know about. Find out what things are older.

7. Why was it necessary for the earth to collect an atmosphere before plants and animals could live upon it?

8. What part of the atmosphere do animals have to breathe in order to live?

Things to Do

1. Gather some pebbles from a stream. Why aren't all the pebbles in the creek smooth? How long do you think the smoothest ones have been there?

2. Look in other books to find out more about how the earth looked long ago.

3. Draw a picture of the way you think the earth looked long ago. Would you have people in your picture? Would there be any skyscrapers in your picture?

Problem 3 · Forces Which Have Changed the Earth

1. A Giant Force Which Tears Down Mountains

The earth is very, very old. It is millions of years old. We have learned that the earth has changed a great deal down through the ages. Tall mountains have been worn away. Other mountains have become taller. Some seashores have been raised and have become the tops of mountains. Others have been buried. What forces are great enough to change the earth so much? There are forces which tear the earth down. There are others which build the earth up.

One of the great forces which tears the earth down is water. You have watched many hard rains. The water went rushing down the brooks and creeks to the rivers. You must have seen the little streams which are formed by the water during the storm. These little streams flow into brooks. The brooks run into rivers, and the rivers into oceans. A little rill of water does not have enough power to change the earth much, but a big, rushing river is a great force.

Mountain ranges are worn down by wind, ice, and water. Notice how round these peaks look. They were once pointed and sharp-looking on top

Do you know that gravity is the force which makes water from the rills and rivers flow into the ocean? Gravity pulls the water downhill. The oceans are lower than the rivers which flow into them.

How muddy streams are after a heavy rain! This is because the water from the rills, brooks, and rivers is carrying a lot of soil along with it.

Water in its effort to tumble and flow downhill forces soil, pebbles, and sometimes even rocks to move with it. From the tiny rills to the large rivers, all are busy carrying the earth from higher places to lower places. The swifter the flow, the more soil and rocks the water can carry. In big floods the water sometimes has so much power that it carries houses, trees, rocks, cars, and other very heavy things along with it.

These rills, brooks, and rivers have been carrying soil and rocks to the sea since the earth was young. For millions of years soil has been scooped out from here and there and carried down to the sea.

The Indians called the Mississippi River the "Father of Waters." It carries more mud along with it into the Gulf of Mexico each year than all the freight trains that go into Chicago each year could carry. More freight trains enter Chicago than any other city in the world. Just think how long the "Father of Waters" has been at work! It was working long before the Indians lived here, and that was a long time ago. When we stop to think of it, it seems strange that we have any dry land left upon which to live. We shall see later why all the land has not been carried out to sea.

It takes millions of years for water to wear down mountains. Each year the water, snow, and ice which come down the mountain sides carry

The Mississippi River drops some of its
soil at its mouth. This soil forms a delta

parts of the mountain with them. Each year the
mountain becomes more worn down.

Scientists call this wearing down, or carrying
away of land, *erosion*. If your class should take a
trip near your school you would be sure to find
places where the land has been worn away. Sandy
places where there are no plants or grass will be
worn away very fast by water.

In some places great canyons, or valleys with

Air Map Corporation of America

The waters of Niagara are slowly wearing the falls back

high, steep sides, have been worn down by water. The Grand Canyon of the Colorado River was dug out in this way. It has taken many years to dig out the soil and rock. It has taken thousands of years for the Mississippi River to wear down its great valley.

Have you ever seen Niagara Falls? The water which goes over the falls is so powerful that it is slowly wearing the falls back. Years and years from now these falls may look quite different, because the force of the water is at work wearing the falls back.

Where does the water go when these clothes dry?

2. Why Water Changes the Earth

You have just been reading about the changes water makes in the earth. These changes all come about because the water of the earth is always moving. It does not stay in the same place for long. If it did, it would not change the earth much. Let us see where water goes and why it keeps moving about.

Have you ever wondered why the wet clothes, which your mother hangs on the line, become dry? Where does the water go while the clothes are drying? It goes into the air. It disappears. This does not mean that the water is gone forever. The water has only changed its form. It has changed from a liquid and gone into the air in the form of vapor.

Water is always leaving the rivers, the lakes, the oceans, and going into the air. It leaves pans which your mother uses for cooking. If you do not believe it, try this. Fill a pan with water. Let it stand in the room for a couple of days. When you look at it you will see that the pan is not so full as it was. Some of the water has gone into the air. When water goes into the air, we say that it evaporates.

Water evaporates faster in warm places than in cold places. If you want to dry your wet mittens when you return from an afternoon of coasting, where do you put them? Would you put them in the refrigerator? If you are in a hurry for the mittens to dry, you will put them near the furnace or in a warm place in the house. The mittens dry while the water in them evaporates into the air. Evaporation goes on all the time, but the warmer the place is the faster the water will evaporate.

Sometimes when your mother puts potatoes on

There was no cover on this aquarium. That
is why the children had to add water so often.
The water in the bowl kept evaporating

to cook and she does not watch them, they burn.
The water that was in the kettle evaporated rapidly because of the heat of the fire.

If you have an uncovered aquarium in your
school room, you may have noticed evaporation
takes place from it. You have to keep adding
water to the aquarium in order to keep it full.

c

You may wonder why water evaporates more quickly on a warm day than on a cold one. Heat causes water to evaporate faster. Warm air can hold more evaporated water, or water vapor, than cold air can. When the air becomes cool again, it cannot *hold* all its moisture. Some of it falls to the earth as rain or snow. When warm air cools it contracts and pushes some of its moisture down. We say that the vapor condenses into rain, snow, hail, or clouds.

When a great deal of warm air cools very rapidly, there is usually a heavy storm. When it cools more slowly, the storm is not a heavy one. Have you ever noticed how much cooler the air is after a very hard storm? Can you understand now why this is true?

"I can't see a thing," said father as he entered the warm house on a cold day in winter. "These glasses are all steamed up again." Father's glasses were not really steamed up. They were covered with condensed moisture. He had been out in the cold. When he entered the house the air was warm. Some of it touched the cold glasses and cooled so quickly that the moisture which was in the air condensed on the glasses.

Sometimes your water glass and pitcher will

The Grand Canyon of Colorado has
been worn down by wind and water

have condensed water on the outside of them. If the water has ice in it and the day is hot, there will probably be condensed water on the outside of the pitcher and glass.

Let us see what it means to have water moving about. When it condenses and falls to the ground, it may fall into a hole and make a mud puddle for boys and girls to wade in.

Some of it may sink into the ground and flow under the ground. It may then bubble out of the hillsides as a spring, where people and animals come to drink.

Some of it may flow under the ground for a longer time, dissolving rocks and making caves.

Some of the water which goes into the ground is soaked up by the roots of plants and used in making food. It then becomes part of the plant until it passes out into the air again through little holes, or pores, in the leaves.

If you have ever been to Yellowstone National Park, you have seen "Old Faithful." It is a geyser which shoots hot water into the air once every hour. This water was probably in the air at one time. It fell to the earth and was heated by hot rocks under the surface of the earth. Then it was shot into the air again.

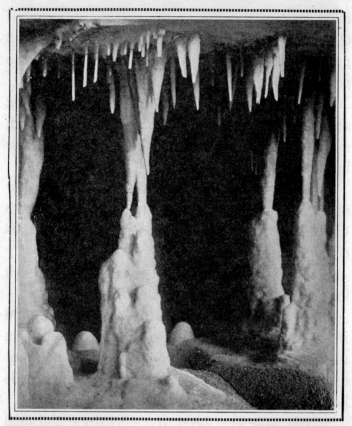

Doesn't this look like fairy land? It isn't fairy land. It is an underground cave formed by water. The hanging things are not icicles. The ones hanging from the ceiling are stalactites. The ones on the floor of the cave are stalagmites

Some of the water which falls to earth forms creeks, rivers, and lakes. This water may be used to turn water wheels as it goes rushing on to the sea.

This is "Old Faithful," a geyser in Yellowstone National Park. Some of the water which is under the ground gets back above the ground through geysers

An old water-wheel mill at Brewster, Massachusetts. This wheel made water work for man

The water which people use in many large cities has been stored in a large lake or reservoir. Sometimes these reservoirs are miles away from the city. The water is brought to the city in very large pipes.

The people in New York City get their water from the Catskill Mountains. Lakes and rivers were dammed and the water from them is stored in large reservoirs. Some of these dams are one hundred and thirty miles from the city. Think of

This is Kensico Dam. It was built to hold
thousands of gallons of water in reserve
for boys and girls of New York to drink

bringing water one hundred and thirty miles in
pipes for use in a city! One of these pipes even had
to cross the Hudson River. A deep tunnel was dug
under the river for the water pipe to go through.

When the water reaches New York it is not the
same as it was when it left the lakes. It looks the
same, but it has had a very important thing done
to it. The New York City Board of Health knows
that the water may not be safe to drink. They
want to be sure that there are no bacteria in it
which will make people ill. For this reason the

water is made pure on its way to New York. A gas called chlorine is added to it at different points along the way. Chlorine destroys the harmful bacteria which, if left in the water, might cause the illness of many persons.

New York also aërates its water supply. That is, the water is shot through pipes up into the air much as it is shot from the hose when you sprinkle your lawn. As the water shoots into the air, the oxygen of the air makes the water still more pure before it falls back into the tank again.

Making water pure is expensive; but pure water is worth all it costs. Before cities made their water supply safe to drink, epidemics of diseases often occurred which caused the death of hundreds of persons. Epidemics of typhoid fever often swept a city because the water was full of typhoid bacteria.

Water is never still for long. It keeps moving about. It evaporates into the air. It condenses and falls to the ground. It hollows out caves; it forms mighty rivers, lakes, and oceans. It forms food for plants and animals. It freezes, and we skate upon it in winter.

It is lucky for us that water does keep circling about. If it just evaporated into the air and never

The camel caravan is still the favorite freight train of the Bedouins in Palestine and Syria. This one is on Jericho Road, between Jerusalem and Jericho. Can you find the water bags which were taken on such journeys?

returned, we should suffer. There would soon be no water to drink, no lakes to swim in, no water to fish in, no water to supply plants with their food. Everything would die without water.

If water just came to the earth and never went back into the air, we should be in trouble, too. At first there would be too much water for plants and animals. It would keep on running until it reached the sea. The lakes, the rivers, the springs, would all run down to the sea. The oceans would become larger.

If you wanted to take a long journey on land you would have to carry water with you as people do now when they travel over the great deserts.

3. How Rivers of Ice Change the Earth's Surface

In Problem Three you read about what happened when a liquid turns to a solid. Can you explain how liquid water turning into a solid has helped to change the earth's surface?

Did you ever hear of rivers of ice? It sounds queer to think of it. But in some places there really are rivers of ice. In cold countries so much snow falls in the winter that it cannot all melt during the short summer. Is this true where you live?

On top of high mountains and in very cold parts of our earth this very thing happens. It is so cold that more snow falls than can melt. The snow gets deeper and deeper. It also gets heavier and heavier. When the top of the mountain can hold no more, the snow starts sliding

When the snow from such mountains as the one you see in this picture starts moving down the mountain sides it is called a glacier

down the sides. This snow has been there so many years that it isn't really snow any more. It has changed to ice. The ice slides down in great rivers. Rivers of ice do not flow rapidly. If you watched one of these rivers of ice you probably couldn't see it move. They move very slowly. Such rivers of ice are called glaciers.

As these heavy glaciers move down the sides of the mountains they scoop out valleys, taking the rocks and soil along with them. These rocks and soil are dropped in other places along the mountain side. Glaciers break off and carry the tops of mountains down into the valleys. Glaciers keep on moving until they come to a place which has a temperature warm enough to melt the ice. Sometimes glaciers do not melt before they reach the ocean. They break off in huge pieces and float in the water. These pieces of ice are called icebergs. Other glaciers melt before they reach the ocean and form lakes and rivers.

Near the north and south poles it is so cold that there is always snow even in the summer time. Many, many hundreds of years ago parts of the United States and Canada were so cold that they were covered with huge masses of snow and ice almost a mile high, which formed glaciers. Scientists called this period the "Ice Age."

Glaciers change the earth's surface in much the same way as water does. They wear away land and carry it to other places. They work more slowly than water. But glaciers can carry heavy rocks farther than water can. They also often pile up dirt and rocks to form dams across river valleys. That is how many of our lakes were formed.

4. Another Giant Force Which Moves Soil

Did the wind ever play a trick upon you? Has it ever snatched your hat off and carried it down the street ahead of you? Just as you were ready to reach out and get it, did another gust of wind come and carry it away again?

Wind is moving air. It can pick up objects and carry them with it. The air is always full of tiny bits of dust which you have seen in the sunlight which comes in through your window. When air is moving slowly it has but little force.

When air moves faster it has more power. It carries larger pieces of soil and other material along with it. During very hard storms, which are called hurricanes and tornadoes, heavy buildings, trees, and other large things are often moved about. In such storms the wind picks up much soil and carries it about. The faster the wind moves the more it can carry. When it slows up, it drops part of its load just as rivers do.

Have you ever lived near, or visited, piles of sand that are called sand dunes? They move about easily. There is usually no grass to hold the light sand in place. Each wind storm moves the sand.

The sands of the Sahara Desert keep bury-
ing the pyramids and sphinxes in Egypt

In deserts the sand dunes move about, too.
Egypt is on the edge of the great Sahara Desert.
Many great tombs in Egypt which kings built
long ago have been partly buried by these moving
dunes of sand.

The air is always carrying some dust and bits
of soil. It carries this dust thousands of miles,
dropping some here and there and then picking
up more. Perhaps some of the dust about your
house has traveled many, many miles. Perhaps
once some of it was in China or in some other
far-off country. Dust is a great traveler.

5. Air Has Force

You have already learned much about air. You know that it can wear away rocks. It can also blow things about. If you remember that we live at the bottom of an ocean of air, you will not be surprised that this is true. All the air above presses down on the air near the earth. It has weight and force.

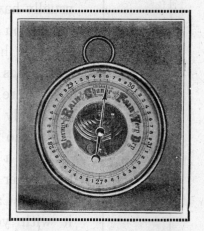

This is a barometer. It tells us how much air is pressing against everything it touches

On some days air is heavier than on other days. This change in the weight, or pressure, of air has a great deal to do with our weather. People who want to find out what the weather is to be look to see what the air pressure is.

Have you ever seen a barometer? Barometers and thermometers can both tell us a great deal about the air.

A thermometer tells us how hot or how cold the air is. A barometer tells us how much the air is pressing against everything it touches. It measures air pressure. When the air pressure gets lighter, we usually have stormy weather. When the air pressure gets heavier, we usually have fair weather.

Do you like to do experiments? Do they help you to understand the things you have been studying? Here is an experiment which will surely have a surprise for you. Do not do it without your teacher.

Find a gallon tin oil can or any other tin can that can be corked. Can you make a dent in it with your hands? Can you dent it with a hammer? You would have to hit it pretty hard to dent it much, wouldn't you? Stand on it. Does it hold you up without denting it?

This is a thermometer. It tells us how hot or how cold things are

Place a board on the can. See if several children can stand on it without denting it. Do you think it would take much force to dent it?

Now put a little water in the can and place it over some heat. Be sure the hole is open for the steam to come out. *Do not cork the can.* Let the

When the children stood on the can it did not cave in

Before the experiment the can looked like the
one on the left. After the experiment it looked
like the one on the right. What happened?

water boil. Soon you will see a white cloud of
small drops of water just above the hole in the
can. This white cloud is formed when the steam
cools and condenses. As it comes out the steam
pushes most of the air out of the can. Is there
any air in the can now?

Steam takes up more room than water does.
When the steam is coming out fast, take the can
away from the fire and put a rubber stopper in
the hole of the can. *Be sure* that the stopper fits
tightly. *Be sure* to take the can from the fire.
Now hold the can under the cold-water faucet.
Run cold water on it. The sides of the can will
crash in with a bang. What made the sides of
the can cave in?

When the can was hot it was filled with steam.
The steam turned back to water as soon as the

can was put in cold water. Water does not take
so much room as steam; so there was nothing but
a little water to fill that big can. The water stayed
at the bottom. The rest was almost empty. The
steam had pushed most of the air out.

There was air outside the can. This air had
force. It had pressure. It pressed against the
outside of the can and made the sides cave in.
Are you surprised to find that air has enough pressure to make this happen?

The ocean of air which is around us has great
force. It works for us.

6. A Giant Force Which Raises and
Lowers the Land

You have been studying about two giant forces
which change the earth's surface. One is air. The
other is water. These two forces are always at
work. They tear down the earth in one place and
add to it in another.

There is still another force at work upon the
earth. It is not a force which tears down. It is
a force which raises and lowers the lands of the
earth. This force works down under the earth's
surface. We can see what it does, but we can
never see the force.

If you want to understand how this force works, you can by playing with blocks. Gather in all the blocks you can find. Get some from your friends. Go to one corner of your room and make a floor with blocks. Fit them together as carefully as possible. Have one edge away from the wall. Now push upon the blocks which are farthest from the wall. What happens? Of course your blocks pile up one on top of another. You have formed tiny hills and mountains of blocks.

You can also see how this force works in another way. Place a piece of paper flat on your desk. Now push one edge toward the other, keeping the edges of the paper on the desk. What happens? Do you have paper hills now?

Inside the earth there are forces which have pushed and pushed in much the same way. They have wrinkled the surface of the earth, making mountains and valleys.

Of course mountains are not made in a few minutes, nor in a few years. It takes millions of years for the mountain-making force to make mountains. It is slow work, just as erosion is slow work. In our short lifetime we should probably never notice that the mountains near us were being wrinkled up. But they are, ever so slowly.

These mountains show that they have been wrinkled

Can you see how these mountains are being worn down?

The holes in these columns were made by the water and tiny sea animals when the columns were under water

Let us see how important this mountain-making force is. If erosion kept on working for ages and ages, much of the land that plants and animals live on would be carried out to sea. The mountain-making force lifts land up higher. It builds up the land that erosion wears down.

Land sometimes sinks, too. Many places which were once above the sea are now below it. Other places which were once below the sea are now above it. The columns in the picture on page 94 have been above and below the water several times. The little holes in them were made by sea animals.

7. How Volcanoes Change the Earth's Surface

You have learned how solids can change to liquids and liquids to solids. Do you remember how we changed ice to liquid? We heated the ice. Ice melts at 32° F. This is really a cold temperature. On a day when the temperature is 32° F. we need a winter coat and mittens to keep us warm.

Rock is a solid, too, like ice. Rock can be changed into a liquid. But it takes a much warmer temperature to melt rock than to melt ice. Rock has to be heated very hot before it melts.

Have you ever seen iron being melted in a very hot furnace? The men who work at the furnace and pour out the melted iron have to work very carefully. The melted iron would burn them badly if they happened to touch any of it. Would melting ice burn you if you happened to touch it?

There are many metals in rock. Iron is one of them. Rock has to be heated very hot in order to melt, just as iron has to be heated. Is there a furnace which heats rock down in the earth?

A few scientists think that some of the center of the earth, which is called the earth's core, is melted rock. Others think it is solid rock made of nickel and iron. All of them are sure that the earth's core is very heavy, and strong enough to hold up the outside of the earth.

There is no fire in the center of the earth. In places the rock near the surface is melted and sometimes flows out over the top of the ground. When the rock comes out of the ground we say that a volcano is erupting.

Volcanoes do not always pour forth melted rock. Sometimes they send out hot gas and steam, too. They are somewhat like chimneys, which let out smoke and gases. Volcanoes shoot forth gases, ashes, and hot melted rock called lava.

Sometimes volcanoes are quiet for hundreds of years. We say that they are dormant, or sleeping. After a long time they may erupt again. Then we say that the dormant volcano has become active. It has awakened from a long sleep. Sometimes these volcanoes stay dormant for so many

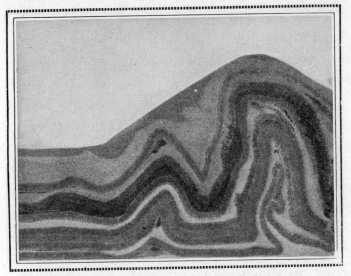

The inside of a volcano might look like this

years that people forget about them and build towns and cities near them. Then, when the volcanoes wake up, lava pours over the cities and buries them. Years ago two old cities in Italy were entirely covered in this way by the volcano Vesuvius.

No one knows just why it is that a volcano sleeps for years and then wakes up. We do know that when a volcano erupts, or wakes up, the chimney which runs down into the earth sends forth melted rock, gases, and ashes. Some force from below makes the volcano erupt. The chim-

Mt. Fujiyama in Japan is a volcanic mountain

neys do not run all the way down into the middle of the earth. They probably go down only a few miles into pockets of very hot rock.

Many of our mountains have been made by lava from volcanoes. Every time the volcano erupts the mountain changes its shape and gets higher.

Look at the mountain of Fujiyama in the picture above. Fuji is a dormant, or sleeping, volcano. It has not erupted for many years. Some day it may wake up again.

Can you see the chimney part of the volcano? This is called the cone of the volcano.

Earthquakes often do damage like this

8. What are Earthquakes?

Have you ever pressed so hard on the two ends of a stick that you broke it? First the stick will bend. Then snap, crack! and it breaks. You pressed so hard on the stick that it broke.

The earth's crust often breaks in much the same way. Of course you couldn't break it with your hands as you did the stick. But there is sometimes so much pressure on the earth's crust that it breaks. First it bends and twists just as the stick did. Then snap, crack! and it slips and breaks.

When the earth's crust breaks, or slips, it makes the earth tremble, or jar. Sometimes the tremble, or jar, is so great that houses shake and tumble over. Sometimes the jar breaks windows and water pipes. Many times the tremble is so small that only a few people notice it.

Scientists call jars like these earthquakes. They say that the earth trembles, or quakes. Our country has had several earthquakes.

In 1923, Tokyo, Japan, had a terrible earthquake. Thousands of people were killed.

During 1930 in Italy there was another very bad earthquake. Many people were killed. Hundreds of houses were damaged.

Many times when there is an earthquake the surface of the earth is changed. Usually there is only a little change. The land may be left with great cracks in it, like the one you see in the picture. It may only be raised or lowered a little.

Today we have learned to build cities in such a way that earthquakes do not do as much damage as they used to.

Things to Think About

1. Why do some rivers wind in and out instead of flowing in a straight path?

2. Where the Mississippi River flows into the Gulf of Mexico it piles up a great deal of soil and rocks. Other rivers sometimes pile up so much soil that they can hardly flow through it. Can you reason out why this sometimes happens?

3. What proof have we that air has force?

4. On windy days it is difficult to walk against the wind. Why?

5. How many forces can you think of that change the earth's surface?

6. Have you ever noticed a rusty color in the water that you use? This color shows that there are minerals in the water. Water dissolves some minerals as it flows through the soil. Some minerals are good for us. Our bodies use them to build teeth, bone, and finger nails. Calcium is one of the minerals which the body needs in order to build strong teeth. It is found in milk, and some vegetables. Milk has a great deal of calcium in it.

 *Things to Do*

1. Make believe that you are a drop of water in a rain barrel. Write the story of your life.

2. Fill in the word or words from the list below which make each sentence true. Do not write in the book.

LIST OF WORDS	
warm	cool
many	erosion
water	glacier
desert	wind
forest	river

a. It has taken _____ years for the earth to change its appearance.

b. Wearing away of land is called _____.

c. Water evaporates more quickly on a _____ day than on a _____ day.

d. A river of ice is called a _____.

e. _____ and _____ are two forces which have changed the earth's surface.

3. Keep a record of the temperature in your schoolroom. Remember that 68°F is about the right temperature for healthy living.

UNIT III

The Air and How it Works

Do you like to do experiments? There are many things you can learn about the air by doing the experiments described in the next few pages. Although you cannot see the air, there is much you can learn about it in this way. You will discover what air is really made of, what causes air to move about, and what moving air, called wind, does.

Problem 1 · The Air We Breathe

1. Of What is Air Made?

Bob had been studying about air. He knew many things about it. He knew that wind was air in motion. He had learned what caused winds. He knew that air had pressure. But still he did not know exactly what air was. One day at school he asked Miss Bell just what air was.

Betty, who was listening, said: "Oh, don't you remember? Air is made up of gases. We learned about that when we were studying about the earth."

"Yes, I remember," said Bob. "It is made of gases. But there are lots of other gases, too. Mother burns gas in our stove. Dad told me that gasoline turns into gas before it is burned in our automobile. I know that air is gas. But is it like these other gases, or isn't it?"

By this time all the children were listening to Bob. When Miss Bell asked if someone could explain about air so that Bob would understand, Alice said: "Air has oxygen in it. Oxygen is the part of air which causes things to burn. Father explained that to me when we were building a bonfire last summer."

c

"Is that all there is of air, just oxygen?" asked Miss Bell.

"No," answered Henry. "I've heard that there is carbon dioxide in the air."

"There is also nitrogen in the air," said Billy.

"Yes, and there is water in the air, too," said Sam.

"I've heard about hydrogen," put in Mary. "Is there any hydrogen in the air?"

"No," said Miss Bell. "There is no hydrogen in the air. Air is made up of many kinds of gases. I will write the most important ones on the board."

What Air is Made Of

Oxygen = about one fifth of the air.

Nitrogen = about four fifths of the air.

Carbon dioxide = only a very little.

Water = sometimes a great deal, sometimes only a little.

"I'd like to know more about oxygen and nitrogen," said Billy. "Can you tell us about them, Miss Bell?"

The children had an interesting time learning about oxygen. Here are some of the things they

These boys are putting out their camp fire before
going home. What are they using to put it out?

learned. They made up this story about oxygen
after they had studied about it at school.

2. Oxygen

Oxygen is a gas. It has more value to us than
gold. We could not live without it. We could do
without gold. We could not live without oxygen.

From the moment we are born until we die
we breathe in oxygen. We breathe it in through
our noses. Then it goes into our lungs. From here
the blood carries it to all parts of our bodies.

Oxygen causes things to burn. You could never have a fire without it. If you want to put a fire out, all you have to do is shut out the air. A blanket thrown over the fire will do it. A pail of sand will also smother the fire, because it shuts out the air.

Usually we do not want to put fires out, that is, the fires which we build for cooking or for warmth. Fire is useful to man. For a long time man did not have fire. He had to eat raw food. He had to dress warmly because of the cold. Fire has helped man for a long, long time. No one knows when it was first made. Remember that if it weren't for oxygen in the air we should not have fire today.

What do you think of the children's story about oxygen?

3. Nitrogen

"Nitrogen," said Miss Bell, "is almost as important to us as oxygen. It is in much of our food."

John laughed. "But, Miss Bell, how can we eat nitrogen? It is in the air. We do not eat air."

"No, of course not," answered Miss Bell. "But we eat food. There is nitrogen in many things which we eat. Some plants, such as clover, are able to take nitrogen from the air. When they die this nitrogen becomes part of the soil. Other plants use this nitrogen. Then we eat these plants."

"Is there more nitrogen than oxygen in the air?" asked Billy.

"Yes," said Jean. "There is four times as much nitrogen as oxygen in the air. Remember that our table tells us that air is about one fifth oxygen and about four fifths nitrogen."

4. Carbon Dioxide

"What else did that table say was in the air?" asked Jim.

"There is a little carbon dioxide," said Miss Bell.

"What good is that?" asked Betty.

"It is very important," said Miss Bell. "Plants use carbon dioxide. They use it in making food. Then we eat the food they have made."

"I thought there would be a great deal of carbon dioxide in the air," said Billy, "because all the animals are giving it out along with their breath. Now I see why there isn't much left in the air. It is because plants use it."

5. Other Things in the Air

"Of course," said Miss Bell, "you have all seen dust in the air. Get where a bit of sunshine comes into a room, and you will be surprised to see how much dust there is in the air."

"There is water in the air, too. When the air gets more water than it can hold, some of its water condenses. We then have rain, snow, dew, or fog."

These are the signs scientists use for the names of gases:

Oxygen = O   Carbon dioxide = CO_2
Nitrogen = N   Water = H_2O

 Things to Think About

1. Miss Bell wrote these questions on the board. The children answered them.

See how many you can answer.

  a. Why will sand put a fire out?
  b. Is there more oxygen or more nitrogen in the air?
  c. What is a gas?
  d. What gas is used by plants in making food?
  e. What gas helps fire to burn?
  f. What gas is carried by our blood to all parts of our bodies?

2. Which method would be more healthful, to dust with a dry feather duster or with an oiled cloth? Why?

Things to Do

1. Find the word in the list below that makes each sentence true. (Do not write in the book.)

LIST OF WORDS			
oxygen	nitrogen	air	clouds
gases	carbon dioxide	dust	scientists

    a. Air is made of _____.

    b. _____ and _____ and _____ are gases found in air.

    c. There is more _____ than oxygen in the air.

    d. _____ is more precious than gold.

2. Try this experiment: Place a short candle on the table. Then light the candle and place an empty glass over it. What happens to the lighted candle?

Problem 2 · How Air Becomes Wind

1. What Causes Winds

Wind is air in motion. It makes things move. It makes the clouds sail across the sky. It throws the great waves of the ocean against the shore. It picks up sand and dirt and carries it for miles. In bad storms it even blows buildings about. In the fall the wind helps the trees get rid of their leaves. It also helps to blow seeds about.

Wind is very useful. In Holland people use the wind to turn large mills which pump water through the canals. Farmers in other countries use the wind for turning windmills to pump water. Sailing boats need wind to blow against their sails and make them move. One very early train had sails on its cars so that the wind would help push it along the tracks.

In China men have sails on wheelbarrows. The sails help the men carry very heavy loads. Can you think of any other ways in which wind is useful to people?

To watch the wind one would almost think it were alive. But of course it isn't. Wind is only moving air. Would you like to learn what makes

In Holland people have built windmills
to pump the water through the canals

air move? If you would, read these experiments
over carefully. Get your teacher or your father
to help you do them. When you have done them
you will understand why air moves.

Experiment 1

Get a small box. A chalk box would be just
right. Get a piece of glass just the right size to
use as a cover for the box. Bore two holes in one
side of the box. Bore the holes far enough apart

Not over bounding billows but bumpy streets. A
taxi wheelbarrow with a sail to help the coolie roll
the conveyance, in the old city of Soochow, China

so that you can place a lamp chimney over each
hole. Place the chimneys over the two holes. Light
a short candle and put it inside the box just under
one of the holes. Next crumple a piece of paper.
Dampen the paper with water. Then light it. It
will only smoke. It will not blaze. Hold this smoking paper over first one lamp chimney and then
the other. Over which one does the smoke rise?
Over which one does it go down into the chimney?

Experiment 1 will tell you what this boy
is doing. You may want to do it, too

The smoke moves with the moving air. Can you
tell why the smoke rises over the chimney which
has the candle beneath it? If you can answer the
following questions, you will know why the smoke
rose:

1. What did the candle do to the air in the chimney?

2. When air gets warmer does it get lighter or heavier?

3. Does warm air rise?

4. Where did the cooler air come from which was
pushing the warmer air up?

Experiment 2

Take a piece of smoking paper to the ventilator in your schoolroom. See whether the air is coming

into the room or going out. If the air is leaving the room through the ventilator, the smoke will go out through it, too. Put a piece of cloth or paper on the ventilator. It will cling to it if the air is leaving the room.

Why does the pin wheel spin so fast when held over the candle?

Experiment 3

You all know what pin wheels are. They turn around fast in the wind. Hold one over a lighted candle. What makes it turn around? Why was the warmed air moving? What was pushing this warmed air up?

2. How Heat Makes the Wind

The sun heats the earth. It makes some places warmer than other places. Most things expand, or spread out, when they are heated. Air is like that. It needs more room when it is heated. The

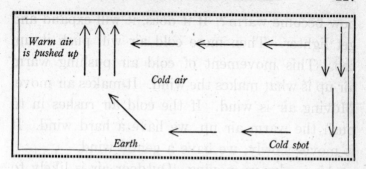

Warm air
is pushed up

Cold air

Earth

Cold spot

Cold air is heavier than warm air.
It keeps pushing the warm air up

air over the warmer places of the earth starts to spread out. As it gets warm it needs more room.

When the warm air expands it also gets less dense. It spreads out in all directions. The more it spreads out, the thinner it gets. There is less air in the same space than there was when it was cooler; so it weighs less for its size.

Now over other parts of the earth the air has not been heated. It is cold. It is heavier than the warm air. It has not expanded. This heavier air pushes in toward the warmer, lighter air because it is heavier than the warmer air. The heavier air pushes the lighter air out. It pushes the warmer air up. The cold air takes its place.

What will happen to the cold air which has pushed the warm air up? Do you think it will now become warm? If it does, it will expand and get lighter. Then more cold air will push it up, too. This movement of cold air pushing warm air up is what makes the wind. It makes air move. Moving air is wind. If the cold air rushes in to push the warm air up, we have a hard wind. If it moves slowly, we have a gentle wind.

Air is always moving. Outdoor air is likely to move more rapidly than indoor air. We do not often feel a hard wind indoors. This does not mean that the air inside is not moving. Air is always moving. Stoves and radiators in rooms help to set the air to moving indoors. Can you see why?

Moving air helps to keep our houses well ventilated. We open our windows to let outdoor air come in and indoor air go out. Which air would probably be heavier in winter? in summer? Why would it push the other air out?

3. What Winds Do

Winds play quite a part in the story of the earth. Sometimes they do good. Sometimes they do harm. When winds are hot and dry they cause crops to die. Sometimes winds blow hard and destroy homes and trees.

Winds do more good than harm. Much of our earth would be a most uncomfortable place in which to live if there were no wind.

 Things to Think About

1. Have you ever been surprised by a heavy storm? You may have been on a picnic and before you knew it you were soaked with rain. The wind blew very hard, too. Can you explain what causes these surprise storms?

2. Why is it that we do not depend upon winds so much as people did three thousand years ago?

3. Try to think of other experiments to do to show that warm air goes up and cold air goes down.

4. When Betty went to bed at half past seven each night she always opened her window from both the top and the bottom. This is the right way to ventilate your sleeping room. The air moves in at the bottom and out at the top. In this way the air is kept moving. Of course we should not sleep in a draft. Just gently moving air is best for us. How do you ventilate your bedroom?

 *Things to Do*

1. Make a list of the harmful things that wind does.

2. Make another list of the helpful things that wind does. Is this list as long as the first list?

3. Draw a plan showing the movements of air just over the radiator in your schoolroom.

Things to Think About

 ## Things to Do

SOCIAL LIFE AMONG ANIMALS: MAN, BEES

UNIT IV
Social Life Among Animals: Man, Bees

Have you ever thought how lonely you would be if you were the only person on earth? Not only would you be lonely, but you would be so busy doing the many things which others now do for you that you would never have time to play, swim, or go on a picnic.

Men have found out that by living and working together life is easier and pleasanter. Other animals besides man live and work together, too. They have a society, or colony, which is very much like the social life which we live. Instead of having fathers and mothers as we do, the bees have queens and drones. They also have nurses, guards, workers, and soldiers in their society. In the following chapters you will find out other ways in which the social life of bees is like the social life of people.

Problem 1 · How People Live and Work Together

Can you count the number of people you know? Do you know a hundred people? Let's see who they are. You know the members of your family. You know the children in your room at school. You know the parents and brothers and sisters of your best friends. You know the children you play with. How many more people do you know?

All the people that you know help each other. Your mother helps every one in your family. She keeps the house in order. She cooks the food and buys your clothes for you. Your father helps your family. He earns the money that keeps your house running. Do the butcher, the baker, and the grocer help you, too?

Think of all the things you would have to do for yourself if you lived all alone. Robinson Crusoe lived alone with only his man Friday to help him. He had to get his own food. He had to build his own house. He had to make his own clothes. No one was there to bring his groceries to him. There was no carpenter on hand to build his house.

Robinson Crusoe had to do everything for himself

There was no tailor there to make him a new suit. He was his own grocer, tailor, and carpenter. His life had to be a very simple one. Do you know why? Robinson Crusoe lived a solitary life on that island. By "solitary" we mean that he lived alone. He had only one friend, and that was Friday. He had to do all his work. No one helped him get his food. No one helped by making him more comfortable. There was no one ready to do kind and helpful things for him. His life was one hard task after another.

How lonely it must have been, staying on that

island day after day, waiting for a ship to come to carry him back to his home! He could not read, because he had no books, newspapers, or magazines. He could not talk on the telephone; there was no telephone and no one to talk to. He could not play the radio, because he had none. He could not play many games with just Friday to play with. Should you like to live as Robinson Crusoe did?

Our lives are quite different from the lonely life of Robinson Crusoe. People living today are social, that is, they are friendly. They talk to one another. They work for each other. They share their fun. In times of trouble they help each other. In fact, people depend so much upon each other that they could hardly get along at all without the help of others.

Think of all the people that work for you every day. The farmer supplies you with eggs, meat, and vegetables. The iceman brings you ice. The milkman brings you milk. The baker bakes your bread. The mailman leaves your mail in your box. The florist supplies you with flowers. The newsboy brings your evening paper. How many more people work for you?

If you live in a city, all the people together form

a big society. This society has a leader usually called a mayor. Many men work for the city. Many of the things which these men do are done for the good of the people in the city. Let's see what a society like this does for its people.

Suppose that your house should catch fire. All you have to do is to find the nearest fire box and turn in an alarm. Soon the firemen from the city fire station nearest you will be on hand to put the fire out.

Suppose you are riding in a car along a busy street. The city policemen and the traffic lights help you to be safe.

Suppose you become ill and need to go to a hospital. A city ambulance will take you there, and a city nurse will take care of you.

If your father lives a long way from where he works, he rides on the city trolley cars, the elevated or subway trains, or the city busses. When your mother goes to shop she may ride, too.

The city garbage trucks gather your garbage every day. The city street cleaners keep your streets clean. The city health department tests the water and milk that you drink, and other foods that you eat.

There are hundreds of things which a city

How many of these people work for you every day?

When harvesting time comes farmers help each other

society does for its people. What other things can you think of that people do for one another?

If you live in the country, your neighbors help you. When your father gets ready to thresh his grain, the threshing machine comes to your house. All the neighbors help, too. It takes a good many men to thresh your grain.

If the road needs fixing, the county road men come to fix it.

The mailman brings your mail to you by automobile or with horse and carriage. You also have a telephone and perhaps a radio.

No matter where you live, other people are always working for you. You could hardly live if you had to do everything for yourself. You would be so busy getting your own food and clothing that you would have no time for other things.

It is pleasanter, easier, and safer for people to live in a society. Should we have had the telegraph, the radio, the airplane, the electric light, the automobile, if men had not worked together?

Could we protect ourselves from bands of robbers if we had no policemen?

Who would make the speed laws if we had no government to make them?

What do you think would happen if everyone did just what he pleased? Should you like to live in that kind of country?

Man is not the only animal that is social. Some of our tiny insects have a highly organized society, too. They have policemen, soldiers, guards, queens, and workers just as people do. The next stories will tell you about some of these social animals.

Things to Think About

1. How many things did other people do in order that you might have your breakfast this morning?

2. What other people handle a letter which the mailman brings to you?

3. Do we do more or less for ourselves than our grandparents did for themselves when they were young?

4. A boy on Clay Street had the measles. The doctor sent a man to tack a red sign on the front door of the boy's house. The man came from the city board of health. How was he helping to keep the city free from disease?

5. In Betty's school the children made some health rules. They were:

    a. Do not come to school when you have a cold.

    b. Place a handkerchief over your mouth when you cough.

    c. Keep your hands away from your mouth.

    d. Use the drinking fountain correctly.

 *Things to Do*

1. Make a list of all the ways in which a city protects the people who live in it.

2. Make a list of the ways in which people who live in the country help each other.

3. Suppose that you lived on an island all alone. Make a list of all the things that you would have to do for yourself.

Problem 2 · Life of Honeybees

1. Wild Honeybees

When I was a little girl living on a farm, my father and uncle used to tell me stories of how to find bee trees. At first I did not know what they meant when they said that they had found another "bee tree." Do you know what they meant?

Wild honeybees build their nests in hollow trees. They build them in tall trees, quite high up the trunk, so that their enemies will not steal their honey.

All summer long my father and my uncle would watch these bees at work storing honey. In the late fall they would take their axes, their pipes, and some good-sized pails and set off for the "bee trees." They would build a fire near one of the trees.

Bees do not like smoke. They do not sting when they are smoked. Wet paper or damp leaves make a very smoky fire.

This is the way my father and my uncle got the honey. They would saw the tree down. The fire would be near the hole where the bees had

This is a bee tree. The men are cutting it in
order to get the honey which is stored inside

their nest. How the bees would buzz! As soon
as they got into the smoke, they became quiet.
Then the men would set to work. They would
take the honey from the nest. When they got
home, my mother would strain the honey. You
see, wild honey is mixed with comb and is not
clear. So mother had to strain it to make it
clear.

Do you know anyone who gets honey that way
now?

2. Why Men Made Homes for Wild Bees

Long ago, in fact so long ago that we do not know just when, man learned to rob the wild bees of their sweet food. They liked the food so well that they thought the bees were almost like gods. They learned to build homes out of hollow logs for them to nest in. Later, men made houses for them that looked like the one you see in this picture. Does it look like the beehives which man makes today?

An old-fashioned beehive

Men were not only interested in caring for the bees in order to get honey. They became interested in their wonderful way of living and working together. Honeybees are very social. They form themselves into a colony. This colony is something like a nation. They have a queen, drones, workers, policemen, health overseers, guards, and nurses.

These children are watching honeybees at work in this observation hive

If you could see the bees at work as these children in the picture can, you would notice that all
of them are not the same size. Some are fat and
short. A great many others are thin, with pointed
bodies. If you looked closely you might see one
bee which is much longer than any of the others.

Drone   Queen   Worker

Three kinds of honeybees. The fat one is
the drone. The long, narrow one is the
queen. The other one is the worker

She would be hard to find, for there is only one in
each hive. You would always find a circle of
other bees around her. By now you may have
guessed who this largest bee is. She is none other
than the queen herself. We call her the queen,
but she is more of a mother than a queen.

Even though these bees do not look alike, they
are alike in many ways. Their bodies have three
parts: a head, a thorax, or middle part, and an
abdomen. The abdomen is the largest part of the
bee's body. They all have six legs. Bees are insects. All insects have three parts to their bodies
and six legs.

The picture shows you the three kinds of bees.
The short, fat one is the drone, or father bee. The

longer, thinner one is the worker bee. The very
long, thin one is the queen. Should you like to
know more about these three bees?

3. The Queen Bee

The queen bee is the mother of the hive. She
lays all the eggs which hatch into baby bees.
Sometimes she lays a thousand or more in one
day. Just think of it! But the bee family is
a large one. There are thousands of bees in a
beehive. Now can you see why the queen has a
circle of guards? She is such an important bee
that the others do not want any harm to come
to her. They keep such enemies as mice, spiders,
and other bees away from her. Is there any person
in our country who has guards to protect him?

4. The Worker Bees

There are thousands of worker bees in each
hive. When you find out all the work they have
to do, you will not be surprised that there are so
many of them. They fly in and out of the hive.
The ones that are coming in have been out getting food.

Do you know where the bees' store is? If you

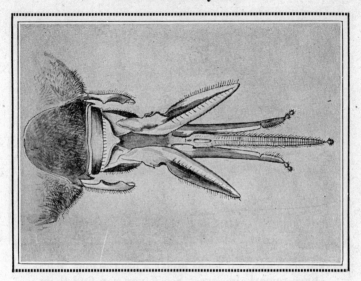

If you looked at the tongue of the worker under
a microscope it would look like this picture

have ever been in a clover field, or an apple or-
chard, or a buckwheat field, or a flower garden,
you have been in the bees' store.

Bees get their food from flowers. The sweet
juice which the flowers hold in their cups is the
bee's food. It is called nectar. Did you ever sip
the nectar which flowers have? It is clear like
water and very sweet. No wonder the bees like it.

If it were not for the very long tongues of the
workers they could not reach the juice. The
flower cups are often down deep in the flowers.

A bee's eye as it looks under a microscope. Bees
have remarkable eyes. See if you can find them

It takes a long tongue to reach so far as that.
Worker bees have long tongues; in fact, their
tongues are so long that they fold them up in a
case when they are not using them.

The picture on page 137 shows you how long a
worker's tongue can be. It folds back when not
in use.

Workers have to have sharp eyes, too, to see
the flowers. Of course it is easy enough to see the
brightly colored ones. But the bees might miss
some of the others if their eyes weren't so wonderful. Every bee has two very large eyes and three

smaller ones. "Five eyes," you say. But that is not all. Each of the two large eyes is made up of about six thousand very small eyes. Instead of two eyes, or five eyes, a bee really has about twelve thousand eyes. In fact, her head looks as though it were nearly all eyes. Can you find the eyes in the picture?

How do you think the workers carry the nectar home? They swallow it. Bees have a honey stomach, or sac. In this sac the nectar is mixed with a juice and changed into honey. When their honey sacs are full, the workers fly home. Upon arriving at the hive the bees spit up the honey and store it in little wax pockets called cells. You will hear more about these cells later.

If you look carefully at bees just returning from a trip to the store, you will see queer humps on their hind legs. Have these bees brought something else home? Indeed they have. These humps on their hind legs are called pollen baskets. They are filled with the yellow dust called pollen, which every flower has. While gathering juice from the flowers the bees also gathered pollen.

You will wonder why they want this yellow pollen. They mix it with honey and make beebread of it. This beebread is what they feed to the baby bees.

Photograph by H. F. Wilson, University of Wisconsin

**Worker bees with their pollen
baskets filled with yellow pollen**

When the workers are making their journeys
back and forth between the flowers and the hive,
they are in danger. Their enemies, the birds, are
always ready to eat them. When danger appears,
the workers get out their spears. "Spears," you
say. Yes, their stings are their spears. They are
at the end of the abdomen. Each spear has ten
pairs of hooks like fishhooks folded along on it.
When the bee tries to pull her spear out the folded
hooks spread out.

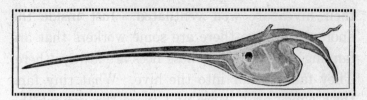

No wonder you shy from an angry bee. This is her sting

When a worker stings you, she sticks her spear into your flesh. It goes in easily. That is not what hurts. It is the poison which is in her poison bag that hurts you. This poison, flowing from the bag and down through a little tube in the sting, goes into your body. It makes your flesh swell up.

Sometimes the bee puts her sting in so deep that she can't pull it out. Off she has to go without her sting and poison bag. When this happens she will never sting again, because she has left part of her abdomen behind her. She dies very soon.

Mud is very good for bee stings. If you should get stung, put some mud on the spot and it will soon feel better.

What a small house the hive is for such a large family! Yes, it is small. That is why it has to be kept so well. Did you ever wonder why bees don't smother to death in the hive? It is because their hives are well ventilated. Just inside the door of the hive there are some workers that are fanning their wings. These bees are always there. They fan cool air into the hive. What tiny fans their wings are! Here and there throughout the hive other workers will also be fanning. There is always a breeze in a beehive. The cool air is fanned in, and the warm air is fanned out. Beehives are often ventilated better than people's houses.

One day while watching bees at work in a glass hive I saw several workers pulling and tugging at a dead bee. They were trying to take it out of the hive. Bees will not live in dirty hives. Every speck of dirt is rolled out by the workers.

Sometimes other insects and worms find their way into a hive. The workers fight the enemy and sting it to death. Then they start rolling and tugging to get it out of the hive.

The workers do other things, too. They are the busiest bees of the hive. Have you ever heard people say that some one was as busy as a bee? They must mean as busy as a worker bee. Would that be busy? You will hear more about the workers later.

5. The Drones

The drones are gentlemen of leisure. They do none of the work of the hive. But they are not to blame for that. They can not gather pollen, for they have no pollen baskets. They can not gather nectar, for their tongues are very short. They are unable to chase enemies out of the hive, for they have no sting. They can not even get their own food. The workers have to feed them to keep them from starving.

In the fall the workers drive the drones out of the hive. They can not feed them all winter. The food supply is too low. Of course you know what happens to the drones. Since they are so helpless, they die. In the early spring you will find no drones in a beehive.

6. The Eggs That the Queen Lays

You may think that the workers are the only bees that are busy. This is not true. The queen is a very busy bee, too. In the early spring she starts laying eggs. She will first stick her head into a wax cell to see that it is ready to receive an egg. If she likes the looks of it she will turn around and back into the cell, leaving an egg

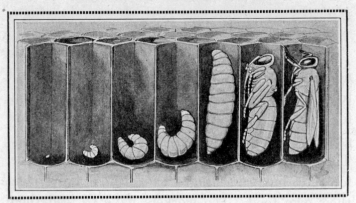

Inside the cells wonderful things are happening

there. The queen's egg basket is in her abdomen. That is why she has to back into the cell. She goes from cell to cell, leaving an egg in each one. Sometimes she lays as many as a thousand eggs in a day.

The queen does not lay all her eggs in the same kind of cells. She lays many of them in small wax cells that have six sides. These will hatch into worker bees. She lays some of her eggs in cells a bit larger. These eggs hatch into drone bees. She also lays a few, just a few, in very large cells. These hatch into queen bees. Most of the cells will hatch worker bees, because more workers are needed in the hive.

Let us keep our eyes on these egg cells. Wonderful things happen inside them. In three days the eggs hatch into white worm-like creatures called larvæ. The larvæ grow very fast. The beebread which the workers supply is good for them. By the ninth day they are full-grown. Then the workers shut them up in their cells. They put a little wax door on each cell. The larvæ now spin cocoons and go to sleep. They sleep about twelve days. At the end of this time they eat the wax caps off their cells and come out as full-grown bees. They are white at first, but by the second day they look like all the other bees in the hive.

7. A Bee Factory

Does your father work in a factory? If so, what does that factory make? People have a good many kinds of factories. Some factories make shoes, others make automobiles, others make food, or clothing, or machines. The bees have a sort of factory in their beehive. It is a wax factory. Should you like to know how this factory works?

The beehive is made up of cells. These cells are made of beeswax. The worker bees make this wax. This is how they do it. For a few days they eat almost all the time. They then go to the top of the hive and hang themselves up by their front legs. In a few hours little wax scales will be seen coming out of their bodies. These are on the underside of their abdomens. The bees scrape the scales off with their hind legs. The scales of wax are then made into comb. Part of the comb is used for storing honey. This is called honey-comb. Part of it is used for the queen's eggs. This is called brood comb.

Many men who raise bees help the bees to make their own comb. They buy wax foundation and place it in the hives. Then the bees make their comb on the machine-made wax foundation.

8. Why Bees Swarm

One sunny day last spring a group of children were out for a walk with me. We were following along a small stream. Soon one of the boys became excited.

"Look, look!" he cried. "What is that all over that tree?"

To our surprise we found that we had come upon a swarm of honeybees. Thousands of them were hanging to a branch. Hundreds were flying about in the air.

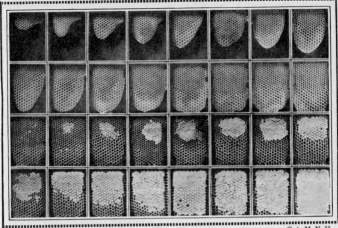

Honeybees make honeycomb of wax. After
the comb is made they store honey in it

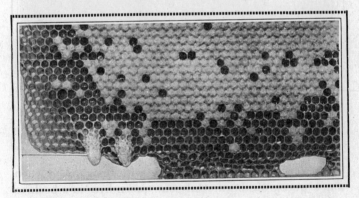

This is brood comb. Notice the two large cells. A
queen bee will come out of each of these. Workers and drones will hatch from the other cells

This swarm of bees left their hive with their queen when
a new queen was born. Only one queen lives in a beehive

Some of the children ran away in fright. Some
rushed to me to be protected. A few very curious
boys went closer to the swarm. I soon brought

all the children near the swarm by telling them that there was almost no danger. Bees that are swarming rarely sting. We sat down at a safe distance to watch this strange sight.

The children had been studying bees in school. They had an observation hive in their room. What fun it was really to see these thousands of bees seeking a new home! Do you want to know why they were looking for a new home?

You remember that the queen bee laid a few eggs in large cells. These eggs hatch into larvæ. The nurses feed the larvæ a kind of food called "royal jelly." How the larvæ grow on this food! When they are full grown they are new queen bees.

Now there can be only one queen in the hive. So when it is time for the young queens to hatch, the old queen takes some of the worker bees and leaves the hive. Some scientists believe that worker bees called scouts go out in search of a new home for the old queen and her swarm. However, no one really knows whether or not this is true.

Usually the old queen leaves the hive before any of the new queens hatch. There may be only four or five new queens to hatch. Then again there may be as many as fifteen or twenty.

As soon as the new queens hatch, they battle to be the real queen. This is the only time queens use their stings. Each queen tries to do away with all the others. If the hive is crowded, one or more of the young queens may swarm out just as the old queen did. Often two or three swarmings take place within a short period of time. At last everything in the hive runs smoothly again. There is only one queen within. The others have either died in battle or have left the hive with their own workers.

Now you can see why the bees which we watched had left their hive. They were swarming. They wanted a new home. We could have caught these bees. Some man did. This is how he did it. He brought a big basket and a sheet. He scooped the swarm into the basket and covered it with the sheet. Then he took them home and put them into a hive.

9. The Wedding Journey

The new queen now makes preparations for a journey. It will be her wedding journey. She makes several short flights before she finally takes the real wedding flight. Some scientists think these short flights help her so that when she takes the long journey she will be able to find her way back to her own hive.

Finally the day for the wedding flight arrives. The drones of the hive go with the queen. They fly higher and higher. Some of the drones are not able to follow. They turn back. The drone that can fly farthest mates with the queen. It is because of this mating that the eggs which the queen lays will hatch into baby bees. So you see the drones are really important at one time of year. They make it possible for new bees to hatch from the eggs which the queen lays.

 Things to Think About

1. Why have men made homes for wild honeybees?

2. What things do the workers do for the other bees?

3. Why is it very important that the queen should be so well protected?

4. What uses does a bee find for its many eyes?

5. Why is it a good thing that two queens will not live in the same hive?

6. Make a list of all the things the bees do to keep healthy. Do we do some of these things, too?

 *Things to Do*

1. Keep watch for a dead bee. When you get one, look at it under a microscope. Look for these things:

    Sting   Pollen baskets
    Tongue   Wings
    Compound eyes

Draw pictures of the way these things look to you under the microscope.

2. If you can, visit a place where bees are kept and watch the beekeeper work with the hives. You may see him smoke the bees before taking away the honey.

3. Try honey instead of sugar for flavoring your food. It is delicious and is much easier to digest.

Problem 3 · Life of Some Other Bees

1. The Bumblebee

Buzz, buzz, buzz! What an angry fellow he seems to be! But you are mistaken. The large, fuzzy bumblebee, though noisy, is almost always a harmless fellow. He will never hurt you unless you bother him. His loud buzz is only a sign that he is busy and happy.

The first warm, sunny days of summer will find the bumblebee on the wing. I should say the mother bumblebee, for the females are the only ones left after the long, cold winter. The male bees all die in the fall.

The bumblebee lives in a cosy, warm nest in the ground all winter. She likes to find a field-mouse's nest in which to spend the winter. Such a nest is just right for her winter home. As soon as the sun wakens her with its warm rays, she starts working. How she does work! If you could see her, you would notice that she was making little balls out of beebread. When she finished making them she put an egg on each one. When the larvæ hatch, they eat their beebread nests.

Cave nest and cells of bumblebees. The nest was
used by a field mouse before the bumblebee found it

They grow fast because they eat most of the
time. They need to eat in order to become bees.

Soon these babies are ready to help their
mother. They make the nest bigger. She needs
more room for her new babies. They are also
able to go on journeys into the fields to gather
pollen and nectar to make into beebread to feed
to the new members of the family.

All that the queen does now is lay eggs. You
wouldn't think she could lay so many. Some

This bumblebee has bored a hole in the
flower so that it can reach the nectar

hatch into workers some into drones, and some
into new queens. These new queens start new
bee families.

The bumblebees are busy all summer gathering nectar and pollen and making honey. By the number you see in the clover field you would think their nests would be full of honey. But this is not the case. Bumblebees are not like honeybees. They do not make honey to save. They make honey to eat. When fall comes there is just enough honey left for the queen to live on during the winter. All the workers and drones leave the supply for the queen and fly away to die.

It is because of this fact that bumblebees have not been cared for by man. Man wants honey for his own use. Since the honeybees supply it, he makes a special home for them.

We should all help protect the bumblebees, however. They help us by carrying flower pollen about. If it were not for them, there would be no red clover. Red-clover nectar is deep down in the flower. It is so far down that the honeybees' tongues cannot reach it. Bumblebees have such long tongues that they can get the nectar. While getting nectar they also carry pollen about from one flower to another. If this pollen were not carried about, the red clover would not produce seeds to make new plants.

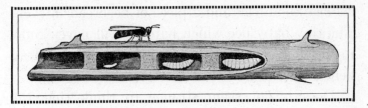

If you could look inside the nest of
the solitary bee, it might look like this

2. Bees that Live by Themselves

Some bees live alone. These bees are called
solitary bees. They build their nests in the ground
or in holes in walls or plants. They use either
earth for building or a sticky resin which they
get from pine trees.

Did you ever get sticky brown pitch on yourself when you tried to climb a pine tree? That
pitch, or resin, is what some of the solitary bees
use for their nests.

The solitary bee almost always builds a row of
cells like those you see in the picture above. In
each cell she places a ball of beebread and an egg.
When the larva hatches, it eats the beebread.

The potter-bee lives by herself. She builds a
little nest with pine resin. How hard she works!
There is no one to help her, because she lives
alone. When she has finished the row of cells,

she leaves an egg and a piece of beebread in each. The tiny baby bee which hatches will never know its mother. In fact, she will probably be dead before the baby has changed into a bee.

Does it not seem strange to think that the baby potter-bees will never know their mother? Even if they flew near her in the clover field, they would not know her. If a baby bee gets into danger it must get out by itself.

The carpenter-bee is solitary, too. It builds its row of cells in the hollow stem of a plant. It leaves a little wall between the cells. What a careful worker it is! A big ball of beebread is left near the egg in each cell for the larva to eat. The mother then rests in the top of the stem and waits for her young to hatch. The bottom egg hatches first. This young bee tears down the ceiling of its cell and waits for the eggs above to hatch. Finally when all are hatched they troop out of the stem, led by their mother.

The leaf-cutter bee gets its name from its habit of making cells for its young out of neatly cut pieces of leaves. It likes rose and lilac leaves best. It may also make its home in the hollow stem of a plant. Sometimes it chooses to make its nest in a keyhole or under a loose board.

The leaf-cutting bee uses parts of rose leaves for lining her
nest. Have you seen rose leaves that looked like these?

Sometimes a leaf-cutter bee uses the tunnel of
an earthworm's home for her nest. She does not
need all of the long tunnel; so she uses only the
top part. It would not do to leave the rest of
the tunnel open; so she blocks it up by making
leaves into screws and fitting them into the hole.
Upon this door of leaves she builds a row of cells,
and lays an egg in each. A bit of beebread is left
for each baby, and away flies the mother.

The mason-bee builds its nest of clay. It fastens it to pebbles in a field. After the cells are
built, the bee gathers nectar and pollen for beebread. Then she lays the eggs. She must protect
her young; so she builds a thick cover over the

top of the nest. The cover is also made of clay. When the young bees are ready to come out, they bore their way through the clay.

Mason-bees often steal each other's nests. If one bee has a nest almost full of beebread and is away getting more, she may find upon her return that her nest has been taken by another bee. The second bee simply lays an egg in it, covers it up, and flies away.

Another bee that steals other bees' nests to lay her eggs in is the cotton-bee. She steals the nests of the carpenter-bees or the mason-bees. Then she lines them with cotton which she gathers from plants. The down on the seeds of the milkweed makes good cotton.

Did you ever find a bee's nest in an empty snail shell? This may seem strange to you, but the resin-bees lay their eggs in snail shells. They close the end of the shell with gravel and resin. Inside the shell they make the cells, or rooms, and lay their eggs there.

Keep watch for these snail-shell nests next summer, when you are at the seashore. They are not hard to find. If you come upon a shell closed with resin and gravel, you will know that you have found one.

Things to Think About

1. In what way is the life of a solitary bee harder than that of a social bee?

2. Where would you look for deserted nests of solitary bees?

3. What flowers do bees like to get their nectar from?

4. What solitary bees are common where you live?

 **Things to Do**

1. Keep your eyes open for leaves that have holes in them. Some will be round. Some will be oval. Find out what caused these holes in the leaves.

2. Get some resin from a pine or a juniper tree. Mix it with small gravel stones. Let it set. Does it get hard? Some bees close the ends of small shells with such resin. Could you use yours for that?

3. Make a collection of deserted nests for your nature museum. Try to find the following kinds of nests:

Nest of the paper wasp   Nest of the carpenter-bee
Nest of the mud-dauber   Nest of the resin-bee
Nest of the bumblebee

UNIT V

Social Life Among Animals: Ants, Wasps, Spiders

1. Life Inside an Ant Hill
2. Life of Wasps
3. Life of Spiders

SOCIAL LIFE AMONG ANIMALS:
ANTS, WASPS, SPIDERS

Life inside an ant hill is a busy one. Ants run here and there carrying bits of food, or eggs, or baby ants from one chamber of their great ant house to another. You will be surprised at the many things ants do.

Have you ever found a wasps' nest? Problem 2 tells a story of some children who found one and cut it in two. They learned many interesting things in this way about wasps and their nests.

You will be interested to read about the clever spider who leaves the neat trapdoor of his house open until he catches a fat, juicy worm or a fly, and then closes it tightly, just in case any enemy should be hiding close by.

Problem 1 · Life Inside an Ant Hill

1. A Picnic

At last the long-planned-for day had arrived. The children in Miss Bell's room were going on a picnic. This was not just a common, everyday picnic. Oh, no! This was to be a very special picnic. The children were going out to find things as well as to eat.

As you know, Charles and Dorothy and the other children in the room were very much interested in science. During the year they had taken trips to see some of the things about which they had studied.

Today was to be another such trip. The children were going to search for ant hills. They had become interested in ants and wanted to learn more about them.

Miss Bell had invited a scientist named Mr. Day to go with them. He had talked to the children at school. They had made a list of the things they wished to learn about ants. Here are the questions they wanted to answer:

1. How many kinds of ants are there?

2. What are ants' homes like?

3. What do ants eat?

4. Do ants have queens, workers, and drones as bees do?

5. In what ways are ant families like human families?

6. What is the special work of each kind of ant that lives in the ant hill?

7. What different kinds of ant hills are there in the world?

The day was a bright, sunny one in June. Miss Bell carried a box of magnifying glasses. Mr. Day had said that they could see many more things if they had glasses. The children had their note-books.

Down the road they walked, looking like a group of hunters about to find game. Suddenly Mr. Day, who was ahead, stopped. Silence fell upon the group. What had he found? The children gathered around a fairly good-sized rock at which Mr. Day was tugging. Over it rolled.

In all directions black ants went hurrying away. "Oh! Oh! Oh!" cried the children in surprise.

"See that one with wings on."

"They are not all the same size."

"What are those little fellows carrying in their mouths?"

Mr. Day is showing the children an ants' nest

Mr. Day and Miss Bell stopped the questioning. They gave the children the magnifying glasses. The children stretched on their stomachs and watched the busy, little, six-legged, black insects at work.

2. Black Ants

"These are the common black ants which we see everywhere," said Mr. Day. "There are thousands, yes, millions of them to be found near your

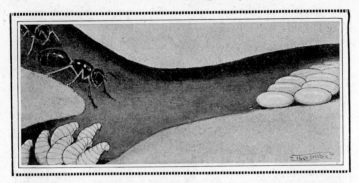

This picture shows the changes that go on inside an ant hill

home. Ants like these were on earth long before man first appeared. Some scientists say ants have been on earth for fifty million years."

"That's a long time," said Charles as he gave a big whistle.

"Yes, a very long time," continued Mr. Day. "These ants have an organized society just as the honeybees do. They have policemen, guards, nurses, queens, workers, drones, farmers, and soldiers."

"Please tell us about the ant hill," said Dorothy.

Mr. Day took a shovel and dug up the ant hill. He cut the hill in halves, leaving one half of it unhurt. This gave the children a chance to look into an ant hill.

The inside of a mound-building ants' nest

"It looks like an apartment house. Look! there's one story on top of another."

"It reminds me of a village," said Charles. "Each room is like a little house. Why do ants have so many rooms in their ant hills?"

"I have told you that ant families are very large," said Mr. Day. "The hill has to be large so that there will be room enough for all." Mr. Day then told the children about the different rooms. Here are some of the interesting things the children learned about the ants and their hills.

o

3. Black Ants and Their Hills

The queen does nothing but lay eggs. After her wedding journey she enters an old ant hill or makes a new one of her own. Then she starts laying eggs. She lays one about every two minutes. The queen lives in one of the many chambers in the underground house. To get to her room you would have to go down a long tunnel. Her room is down deep so that she will be better protected. Do you remember that the queen bee had guards? The queen ant has guards, too. They see that no harm comes to her.

The queen is a very large ant. She has a big abdomen, for she keeps her eggs in it. Before she goes on her wedding flight she has wings, but when she returns she bites them off. From now on she does nothing but lay eggs, and eggs, and more eggs. Some queens go on laying eggs for ten years. Think how many they must lay in that time!

What are those little ants doing? They are carrying the tiny eggs out of the royal room. The eggs are the size of a pinhole. Let's follow the ants. Out into the main tunnel, or hallway, they go. Now they turn into a room full of eggs. They keep the eggs moist so that they will stick together. When the workers or nurses wish to carry them to another room they can carry many at a time. This saves time and labor for the worker ants.

The eggs are soon carried from this first egg room to another one which has older eggs in it. This room is nearer the top of the hill. The eggs need to be kept warm. The rooms nearer the top are warmer than those deeper down because the sun warms them.

It takes about two weeks for the eggs to hatch. During this time they are moved from one room to another. When they hatch into larvæ they are put into another room. Here you will see many nurse workers. These are the middle-sized workers. They feed the larvæ "honeydew" or "ants' milk." Ants get this liquid from their cows. You will learn more about the cows later. The nurses put their mouths close to the mouths of the larvæ, who gobble up the food. You would think the larvæ would never stop eating!

The larvæ grow fast and are soon ready to spin their cocoons. They are taken to still another room and buried in the sand. There they stay buried while they spin their cocoons and change from white larvæ into ants.

4. Kinds of Ants

Not all the ants which hatch look alike; in fact, five different kinds will hatch out. There will be a few large-sized queens. There will be a good many drones, or fathers. There will be three sizes of workers. The tiny ones are the workers which clean the hill. The middle-sized workers are the nurses. They feed the queen and care for the larvæ. Then there are the large workers. They are the soldiers and guards. They act as watchmen, watching for enemies and keeping them out of the hill. They protect the rest of the colony when enemy armies come to rob their hill. The rooms at the top of the hill are the homes of these soldiers.

5. The Ants' Cows

"Please tell us about the ants' cows," begged Betty. "It seems funny to think that ants keep cows. What are their cows like?"

"The ants' cows are aphids (a'fidz). They are tiny plant lice. You can see them eating the juices out of leaves or roots of plants. The ants think so highly of their cows that they make a home for them. They collect the aphid eggs, and when

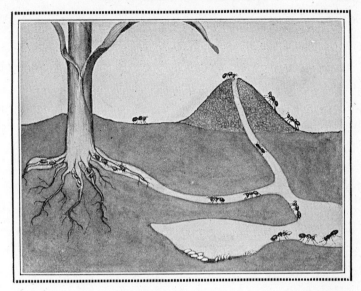

The ants' cows, or aphids, feed upon trees and other plants

they hatch, feed them just as they do their own larvæ. From the aphid room the workers build tunnels to the roots of weeds and vegetables or trees. Here the aphids live, sucking the sweet juices from the plants.

"When the ants want milk they stroke the aphids with their antennæ. Antennæ are long feelers which grow on the ants' heads. When stroked, the aphids give up their milk, or honeydew. What an easy way for the ants to get their food!"

Hundreds of queen ants take wing upon their wedding flight

6. The Wedding Flight

"Please tell us something about the wedding journey," asked Betty.

"Of course I will," said Mr. Day. "It is an interesting sight. If you watch closely in the spring you may make a discovery. On one certain day all the queens and drones leave their ant hills. It is their wedding day. For a while they stay on the ground. Then, as if by some unseen sign, they spread their wings and fly into the air. Hundreds, yes thousands, of them set sail. Each queen mates with a drone. They are not careful of the

family of ants with which they mate. A queen
from one hill often mates with a drone from
another.

"Soon the queens come to earth. They look
for ant hills. If they are not lucky enough to
find an old one they set about building a new one.
These new hills are very small. There is really
only one room at first. The first larvæ are fed by
the queen herself. She feeds them honeydew from
her own mouth. When the first tiny workers are
big enough to work they make the hill larger so
there will be enough room for the new ants which
will soon hatch."

7. Red Ants

"Aren't there other kinds of ants besides these
common black ants?" asked Charles.

"Yes, there are the large red ants which are
enemies of the black ants," said Mr. Day. "They
organize armies and make war upon the black
ants. This is how they fight. First, a few soldiers
who have been sent on ahead will arrive to make
plans for the fight. They will go away and return
again with an army of red soldier ants. These
soldiers circle around the hill. A few go down into
the hole. Back they come with a bundle of larvæ

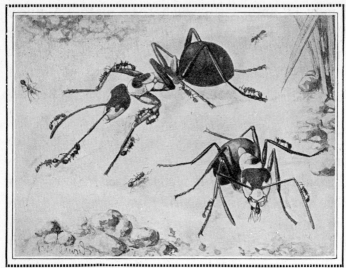

These red ants have been battling with the black ants.
They are now returning home with their prisoners

or eggs. Some thousands of black ants come out loaded with their eggs. They try to break through the enemy's line. Alas! The enemies attack them and rob them of their eggs.

"After robbing the black ants, the soldiers carry the larvæ and eggs home."

"What do they do with them?" asked John.

"They do two things with them. Some of the eggs and larvæ are used for food. Full-grown ants are made into slaves. They do all the work for their masters. In fact, the red masters sometimes

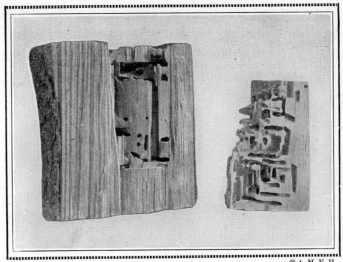

Carpenter ants build nests in stems of plants

become so lazy that if they lose their slaves they die because they are no longer able to work for themselves."

8. Farmer Ants

"Some red ants are good farmers. They build rooms in their houses for gardens. Into these gardens they carry leaves. The leaves are kept damp. Tiny little plants grow on the leaves. These tiny plants are used as food. The gardener ants live in Texas and in South America.

"Still other ants make rooms called granaries, in which they store seeds. They build very good roads leading to the farmers' grain. Back and forth go the ants, carrying kernels of grain and storing them for food in their granaries. Do you think these ants could be called farmers?"

9. Carpenter Ants

"Are there some more kinds of ants?" asked Betty.

"Yes, hundreds more. In fact, there are three thousand different kinds of ants. The carpenter ants nest in wood. They bore holes in posts or trees and build their nests there. These ants have destroyed many posts, beams in houses, and trees. They make them soft and useless."

10. White Ants

"In hot countries there are many white ants, called termites. These white ants do much damage. They eat through wood, destroying parts of houses. If they get into a library they will eat the leaves of the books. It is very difficult to keep these ants away from books. Library buildings are now being made of stone or concrete so that the ants cannot eat their way in.

"The houses of the white ants are different

The termites build huge nests like these

from common ant hills. Some are large mounds.
Others are hard towers which are sometimes ten
to eighteen feet high. Still others look like toadstools. These nests are found only in Africa."

11. The End of the Trip

As the sun got low in the western sky the children started back home. Their heads were full of
all the new things they had learned about ants.

As they walked along they checked to see how
many of the questions on their lists they could
answer. Miss Bell was surprised at all of the questions they could answer.

"Good night, Miss Bell," they said as they left the school house. "This has been the best trip of the year."

 Things to Think About

Mr. Day sent the children some questions to answer. Can you answer them?

1. What different kinds of ants do you know about?

2. What does an ant hill look like?

3. How do red ants get their slaves?

4. Why would termites, or white ants, be pests?

5. In what ways is an ant colony like a bee colony?

6. Make a list of special ants in an ant hill which are like special people in our own society.

 *Things to Do*

If you would like to watch ants build their tunnels, go for a walk in search of an ant colony. Take a shovel and a glass jar with you. When you find a hill dig deep into it with your shovel. Put the ants and some dirt into the jar. The queen lives down deep in the hill, and unless you get a queen your ants will all die. Set the jar in a pan of water so that the ants can't escape. Feed them bits of bread and sugar, and keep the dirt moist. Soon the ants will be building tunnels against the sides of the jar. It will be fun to watch them work. If you keep them in the dark part of the time, they will work better.

Problem 2 · Life of Wasps

1. Wasps That Live Together

Betty and Jack came to school one day in winter with a big gray thing in their hands. Their eyes were shining. They seemed breathless, as they often did when they were about to show a great treasure.

"What's that?" called several children as they gathered round.

"You shall see," said Jack.

"My father and I went over to the little old house where we used to live. We hadn't been there for several months. We found this big gray thing hanging on the beam in the kitchen."

"But what is it?" they begged.

It was Betty's turn now. "It's a paper wasp's nest. Father said it was the nest of the hornet. He said that it was safe to bring it to school now because all but the queen wasp had died. You wouldn't dare take one down during the summer. You would have thousands of angry, buzzing wasps after you if you did."

"What do you suppose it looks like inside?" asked Mary.

"We must find out. Let's look at the outside first, though," said Jack.

The children set about to discover how the wasps

© A.M.N.H.

This is the nest found in the old house. Who made it?

got into their gray paper house. Down at the bottom they found a little opening. Miss Bell told them that the opening was at the bottom so that water could not damage the nest.

"The outside is very tough. I wonder what it is made of. Do you know, Miss Bell?" asked Jack.

"Yes, these wasps make their houses of paper. What's more, they make their own paper," said Miss Bell. "Wasps have been making paper for ever so much longer than people have. They mix bits of wood with a liquid which comes from their mouths. They chew and chew it until it is just right. Then they put layer after layer of it into their houses."

"Let's look inside," said Betty.

The children decided to cut open the nest so that they could see what the inside was like. It took a big knife to do it. Miss Bell cut it while the children watched.

"Oh! Oh! Oh! How funny," they cried as they saw the inside of the interesting apartment-house nest. There were stories, one above the other.

"It would hold hundreds of wasps, wouldn't it?" asked Charles.

"Yes, even thousands," said Miss Bell.

Upon looking closely the children found row after row of empty cells.

©A. M. N. H.

When the nest was cut open it showed layers of cells like those you see in this picture

These had been the homes of the baby wasps.

"I should think the babies would fall out, because the cells are open at the bottom," said Betty.

"The queen takes care of that," answered Miss Bell. "She fastens the eggs to the roof of the cell.

Then when the larvæ hatch they fasten themselves to the roof, too."

"Where are all the wasps now?" asked Jack.

"In the fall the wasps die. The queen is the only wasp that lives through the winter. She has to raise a whole new family every year."

"I saw one nest of this kind hanging on a tree once last summer," said Bill. "The wasps that lived in it were yellow and black."

"That is the yellow jacket's nest," said Miss Bell. "They are paper wasps, too. They make the same kind of nests as the brown and the black wasps. They are very saucy fellows. If you are wise you will leave them alone. For although they are friendly to each other, they do not like to have outsiders bother them."

The children kept the wasp's nest. They put it into their museum. Do you have a museum where you put your treasures? It is a fine thing to have.

2. Wasps That Live by Themselves

Last summer my brother Bob and I spent several weeks of our vacation on a farm. Every day we went for walks about the country. Some days we went along the edge of a beautiful clear stream.

On other days we wandered through the woods. We were always looking for excitement, and it never failed to come. The day we saw the mother oriole teaching her babies to fly was a red-letter day. One day we came upon a robin fighting to drive a snake down from her nest. What a fight it was! Then another day we made this discovery.

We were seated on the sandy shore of a stream. Both of us were busy eating the lunch we had brought. As we sat there we discovered a little black insect. She did not seem to mind our watching her. She was too busy even to notice us. Back and forth she was flying. We soon found out that she was a wasp. Later we learned that she was the mud-dauber.

As she worked we learned many new things. The mud-dauber was building herself a house. First she flew to the water's edge and got a bit of mud. This she rolled into a ball. As she flew she mixed the mud with a bit of juice from her mouth. Later on we found out that this juice acted somewhat like cement. It made the mud hard.

Next she flew to a dry spot. It was here that she was building her house. It was fastened to some flat stones lying on the ground. We watched

c

her closely. She had already finished three tiny rooms and was building a fourth. The rooms were

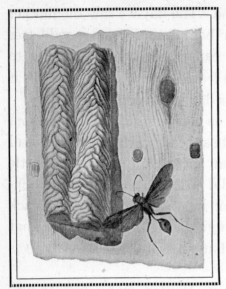

A mud-dauber builds a nest like this

deeper than they were wide. They were about an inch and one-half deep. Back and forth she flew until the fourth room was finished.

"What do you suppose she will do now?" whispered Bob.

"Wait and see," I answered. We hadn't long to wonder. She went scooting off among the high grass back from shore. This time she did not fly. She walked. We lost sight of her; so we had to wait for her return. Before long back she came dragging a dead caterpillar. How she ever managed it was a wonder to us. But there she was with a caterpillar three times her size.

We found out later that the caterpillar was not really dead. She had only poisoned him a little so that she could drag him home with her. She rolled the caterpillar into one of her newly built rooms, and it fell to the bottom.

We were breathless by now. Our eyes were wide open, and in a little while we saw the mud-dauber lay an egg on top of the fat caterpillar. So that was it! The caterpillar was to serve as food for the wasp's baby. Quite an idea, we thought.

She brought more mud and closed the doorway to the cell. Off she went for another caterpillar. But when she returned she was dragging a spider, instead. It seemed that if she couldn't get a caterpillar she would take a spider.

In an hour she had finished. The cells were filled and closed. Off she flew. We never saw her again. But each day or two we returned to the spot. Some things were happening inside those cells. Of course we could not see it, but we knew that each egg would hatch into a larva. The larva would eat and eat until it was sleepy. Then it would spin a cocoon, and while it slept it would change into a wasp like its mother.

One day about two weeks later we were lucky enough to be there to see two of the baby mud-daubers bite their way out of their cells, stretch their wings, and fly off.

We had become so interested in wasps by this time that we kept on reading about other kinds.

These jugs are the homes of two mason-wasps

Here are some things we found out.

There is a wasp called the mason-wasp which builds its mud house on the branch of a tree. Its nest looks like a jug, but it opens at the bottom instead of at the top. The outside is made waterproof by the same sort of cement that the other wasps use. The juice from wasps' mouths acts like cement. The mason-wasp provides caterpillars for its young.

How we wished we might be lucky enough to find a nest of the cicada-killer wasp! It is the largest of the solitary wasps. It hunts for locusts, or cicadas, for its babies.

The home of the cicada-killer wasp is eighteen inches deep. It has rooms which open into a tunnel or passage-way. Into these rooms the wasp puts the locusts, and lays her eggs on them.

It is hard work for the killer wasp to get the cicada home

These cicadas were dragged here by the killer
wasp. They will be eaten by the wasp's babies

Perhaps you may have a chance to find the nests of some of these wasps. If you do you will have great fun watching them work. You will find out many new things about them.

All these wasps live alone. There are some wasps that live in colonies. There is a story in this book about the wasps that are social. Have you read it?

 Things to Think About

1. Why have men made houses for honeybees and not for wasps?

2. Why can't solitary bees provide honey for man to use?

3. The first wasps that hatch in the spring are workers. Of what use are they to the queen?

 *Things to Do*

1. Try to find an empty wasp's nest. Tear it apart carefully. Notice how the layers of paper are put on. Look at the rows of cells. If you cut through the middle of the nest, from top to bottom, you can see the rows very well. Look carefully at the opening. Why is it at the bottom instead of the top of the nest?

2. Watch for dead wasps. Look at them carefully under a microscope. Draw a picture of the way the parts look to you under the microscope.

Problem 3 · Life of Spiders

You have been learning many things about social and solitary insects. Let us now take a look at still another family, the spiders. These creatures are not insects, for they do not have three parts to their bodies, nor do they have only six legs.

Spiders are arachnids. They are related to insects, but they are not insects. Spiders have only two parts to their bodies — a front part, which is really the head and thorax, and a back part, which is the abdomen.

Instead of six legs, spiders have eight, which grow from the front part of their bodies.

There are many kinds of spiders. Most of them are solitary. They do their own work and let the others look out for themselves. They do not help one another. If a spider gets into trouble she must get out of it all alone. When she wants food she must capture it alone. Wait and see how she does it. Some mothers pay no attention to their children. Others spend their lives watching over them. There are very few families of spiders that live a social life. Let us learn more about these interesting creatures.

SPIDERS THAT SPIN WEBS

1. The Banded Spider

As you have probably guessed, the banded spider gets its name from the colored bands that cross its body. These bands are yellow, black, and silver. The banded spider is fond of small insects and flies, and builds a spiral web in which to catch them. Because this spider is found so often in gardens, it is sometimes called the garden spider.

The web is spun from fine silk thread which the spider makes in its own body. It is made by spinnerets, which are on the under side of the abdomen of the spider. The silk is a liquid while it is inside the spider's body, but it becomes hard and strong as soon as it comes out into the air.

How the banded spider works to make its web! No wonder it is willing to work so hard, because the web is the spider's hunting trap. First threads must be fastened to twigs or branches which are near each other. Then straight threads are sent out from the center. These threads are like the spokes of a wheel running out from the center, or hub. The spider makes more than twenty spokes for her web wheel. Next a spiral of thread is spun from the center to the outside of the web. This

Web of banded garden spider. What
do you think she is waiting for?

spiral is fastened to each spoke of the web to keep
it in place and to make it strong. Finally the
banded spider puts on her trademark. This is a
zigzag band of silk running from the center to the
bottom of the web.

As soon as the web is completed the spider
seats herself quietly in the center and waits. Any
bug, beetle, or fly that happens to fly that way
suits her.

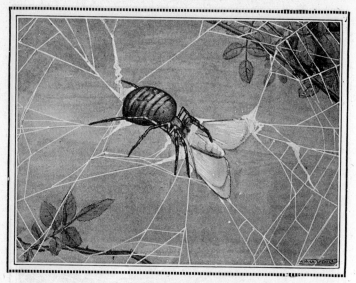

Just to be quite sure, the banded
spider wraps her prey in a silken sheet

The spider does not see her food as it flies into
the net, for even though she has several eyes, they
cannot see far. She feels the web moving back
and forth as she sits in the center. You may be
surprised to know that she feels with her eight
legs. On each of her legs she has hairlike spines
with which she feels.

You would think that the web was enough of a
trap, but the banded spider doesn't think so. She
starts spinning more silk, which she makes into a
white sheet. With her hind legs she wraps the

Photograph by Hugh Spencer

The garden spider has just finished this egg sac.
It holds the five hundred eggs she has just laid

trapped victim in the newly made sheet. When all movement stops, the spider goes near the prisoner.

Just to make sure that her prey dies she sticks her poison fangs into its neck. This poison kills it at once. Now she is ready to feast upon the blood of the victim. She wants nothing but the blood; so she throws the rest away. Then back she goes to the cushion in the center to wait for another victim to fly her way.

Not only can this spider spin a web and a sheet, but she can also spin a silk bag in which she lays her five hundred eggs. The bag is balloon-shaped and is fastened to twigs and weeds. Inside

These young spiders are flying to their
new homes in their silken airplanes

the bag she spins silk. On the outside she makes a
waterproof silk covering to protect the eggs.

After working so hard you would expect the
garden spider to watch over the silk balloon and
protect the eggs. But she does nothing of the
kind. She has used up all her silk. She can no
longer spin a web to catch more food. So she dies.

Several winter months pass by. The eggs hatch
into young spiders. They stay inside the balloon
until they are about four months old. Then one
day the hot sun cracks the balloon open, and out
shoot the many spiders. These babies climb to

the tops of the nearest twigs and start spinning silk thread.

As the silk threads float in the breeze they break and fly away, carrying the spiders along to their new home. These threads are the airplanes of the spiders. They carry them for miles if the wind is strong.

2. Other Web Spinners

There are other spiders that spin webs in which they trap their prey. The triangular spider does this.

She spins a triangular shaped web as the banded spider does, but instead of staying in the center she seeks a hiding place a few inches away.

Leading from the spider to the center of the web is a silk thread. You will wonder what this is for. First of all, it is the bridge upon which the spider goes back to the web. It is also a telephone wire, which carries a message something like this, "Come quick, a fly has fallen into your trap." Of course the thread does not really say its message in words. All it does is shake back and forth. The spider listens to make sure it is not just the wind; then over the bridge she rushes to get her victim.

3. The Grass Spider

Not all spiders spin spiral webs. The grass spiders spin quite a different kind of home. They spin a large sheet of silk which they fasten to spears of grass. At one side of the sheets they build funnel-shaped tubes, which serve as hiding places for the owners of the webs. As soon as they spy an insect caught in their silk-sheet webs they run up the funnel-shaped tubes and seize it. The tubes have openings at the bottom which offer the spider a means of escape should an enemy enter from the other end. Many people call these grass spiders funnel-web weavers because of the funnel-shaped tubes in their webs.

SPIDERS THAT DO NOT SPIN WEBS

Not all spiders catch their food by spinning webs. Some use an easier method. Let us see what these spiders are like.

1. The Jumping Spider

These spiders jump for their food. They steal about quietly. Their eyes are sharp. Every few steps they raise their heads and look about. You

This crab spider is waiting for its supper to appear

may have had one of these spiders stare at you. When they see a fly, a beetle, or a bee they spring upon it. Their short stout legs enable them to jump a long distance.

2. The Crab Spider

Crab spiders get their name from their habit of walking sidewise as many crabs do. These spiders hide in flowers waiting for a bee or a butterfly to come for its sip of nectar. Their color is so much like the flowers that they are not easily seen. In fact, some of the crab spiders have the power to

change their color from yellow to white so that
they will match the flowers upon which they rest.
With a quick sidewise run they stick their fangs
into their enemies and then feast upon them.

When it comes time to raise a family, the crab
spider stops hunting for food. She has more important business to see about. She spins a tiny,
thimble-shaped bag in which to lay her eggs. Very
carefully she covers it with a tight-fitting lid.
Above it she makes a lookout place, or watch
tower, for herself.

Here she sits day after day guarding her nest
of eggs. She frightens away every creature that
comes near. In about five weeks she makes a hole
in the nest so that her family may get out, and
then she goes off to die.

The young spiders climb up high on a twig.
They begin spinning their flying-machine threads,
which are soon to break away and carry their
pilots to a new home.

3. The Tarantula Family

You may have been told that spiders are poisonous. This is true in a way. Spiders have poison
fangs. They use them to kill the animals which they

eat. But most spiders are harmless to people. If a spider bites you, it is usually about like a bee sting.

There is one spider family which has strong poison. This family is known as the Tarantula (ta răn'tū la) family. They are found in warm parts of our country and are the giants among spiders. They live in burrows in dry, stony ground. These burrows are about a foot deep and an inch wide. At the entrance the spider builds a mound of straw, stones, and sand.

Here she sits sunning herself and watching for her dinner to arrive. A fat bumblebee just suits her. When one arrives she sticks her poison fangs into its neck, which kills it at once. Then what a feast she enjoys!

You would not expect this cruel hunter to be a good mother, but she is. When August comes she spins a thick, silken bowl like a tent. After laying her eggs upon it, she rolls the tent into a small ball about the size of a cherry. She fastens the ball to her spinnerets and keeps it there until the eggs hatch.

Even then she does not leave the young spiders. No, indeed! They climb upon her back and ride about wherever their mother chooses to take them.

What an easy way to see the world! you say. Perhaps so, but it is a crowded way too. Imagine

How would you like riding as these
babies are upon their mother's back?

a great many baby spiders on top of the mother
spider's back. They have to hang on tightly, or
else they will fall off. By the end of five or six
months they would probably rather walk than
ride in such a crowded coach.

Besides, they are hungry. They have had no
food during this long ride. The mother caught
food for herself, but she never bothered about
feeding her family. They just lived upon the
food which they had in their own bodies. Since
they had no other food, they did not grow.

Finally all of the young ones get restless.

The nest of the trapdoor spider
comes in handy when danger is near

Up they go to the top of a twig. Away they fly in their flying machines.

What does the mother do after her family leaves? She does not die, as so many other mother spiders do. She starts hunting in earnest. Soon she makes another tent and lays more eggs.

4. The Trapdoor Spider

One of the tarantulas makes a trapdoor at the entrance to its burrow. The hole is almost always dug on a sidehill, and the hinges to the trapdoor are on the uphill side. When a spider wishes to come out, she lifts the door from within. When she wishes the door closed, it is quite a simple matter. The weight of the door itself closes it. Should an enemy try to open the door, the spider bolts it from the inside by placing its claws in certain holes in the door. These holes are on the downhill side; so the door is held firmly on both sides.

5. The Social Spiders

The spiders you have been reading about have not been very social. They have built their own webs, caught their own food, and made their own egg baskets. There was not much working together — one worker did not help another one.

Most spiders are solitary. There are, however, three kinds of spiders that are social. They all belong to the same family, and they are found in Africa and on the islands near there. When these spiders hatch they do not go off alone. Instead they all stay together. They make a web net, which sometimes covers a whole tree. It is not a spiral web like those you have seen so often. It is a net of threads woven this way and that in order to catch insects, much like the nets we use to catch minnows in.

Sometimes as many as one hundred spiders live in this one nest. Whenever an insect strikes the net, numbers of spiders run to capture it. Then all the family feed upon it together. Each shares with the others.

 Things to Think About

1. How are spiders different from insects?

2. Name the spiders that spin webs.

3. In what other ways do spiders catch their food?

4. What wasps must the spider be on the lookout for?

 *Things to Do*

1. Catch a spider in a bottle and put it into a wire cage. Put in a fly or beetle for it to eat. Watch the spider build a web. Break some of the threads of the web and watch this busy worker mend them.

2. In the spring try to find the balloon-shaped nest of the banded spider. Bring it to school and watch the babies hatch. They will make their flying machines for you to see. Then let them go.

UNIT VI
How Other Animals Live

What busy workers beavers are! They are carpenters, engineers, and lumbermen. As carpenters they build their clever, two-story lodges, or houses. In order that their lodges may be safe, they must put them in a pond which they have made by building a dam across a stream. As you know, only engineers can build dams. As lumbermen the beavers cut down trees with their sharp teeth to use in their building.

Beavers work together just as bees and wasps and people do. All animals that work together are called social animals. Some animals work together all of the time; others for only a part of the time. The following stories will tell you why.

Problem 1 · Life of the Beaver

1. A Mammal

The bees and ants you have been reading about are old friends of yours. They are easy to find because they live all around you. It is easy to watch them work.

Beavers are not so easy to find. They are shy animals. They have so many enemies that they do much of their work by night. You will not be likely to see a beaver at work.

In some ways beavers are much like ants and bees and men; that is, beavers are social. They live and work together. They help each other in getting food.

There is one way that beavers are different from ants and bees. Beavers are mammals. Bees and ants are insects. Mammals do not hatch from eggs as insects do. The mammal mothers feed their babies upon milk from their own bodies. Do insects do this?

Beavers are water-loving animals. Their webbed hind feet make them very good swimmers. They cannot travel fast on land. When they walk about they waddle. Although beavers can live in water,

Gnaw, gnaw, gnaw! The tree will soon topple over. Can you see what the beaver will use it for?

they cannot stay under water all the time. They have to come to the top to breathe every four or five minutes. If they breathed through gills as fish do, they could stay under water. But of course they couldn't live on land either, if they breathed as fish do. They go to the shore only in order to cut down trees and bushes which they need for food or for building their dams and lodges. The rest of the time they spend in the water.

Beavers are really very interesting animals. They do things which are very difficult. This story will tell you about some of the things beavers do.

©U. S. Biological Survey

Here is a beaver dam

2. How Beavers Build Dams

Beavers must live in water. They have enemies. The wolf, the bear, the wild cat, the fox, the hawk, and sometimes man, are enemies of the beavers. When on land they are always in danger.

When beavers look for a place in which to build a home, they always pick out a stream. The stream may be small or large. They set to work building a dam. The dam makes a pond for them. They want a pond large enough for protection. They begin work at once. They gather branches of willow, alder, or birch from the trees near the stream.

Ash stump gnawed by beavers. What
sharp saws their teeth must be!

Their sharp teeth are their saws and axes.
Their broad tails hold them steady while they
saw. Gnaw, gnaw, gnaw, they go until the trees
are cut. Gnaw, gnaw, gnaw, they go until the
branches are sawed off. They carry them in their
teeth to the edge of the water. From there the
branches float to the right spot for the dam.

The beavers push these branches into the mud
at the bottom of the stream. The thick ends of
the branches are placed upstream. Then the busy
workers pile sand, gravel, and stones on top of

©A.M.N.H.

The beavers have been at work on these trees

the branches to hold them fast. They dig up the mud from just above the place where they are building the dam. This makes the pond deeper.

How hard they work! Layer after layer of branches is piled one upon another. Layer after layer of mud is put upon the branches. At last the dam is high enough. At first it leaks. But the water carries more mud into all the cracks until it becomes water-tight.

You might think that now the beavers' work on the dam was done. Not a bit of it. They must keep it in repair. Whenever a flood comes, the dam will need fixing. Every time there is a new leak, the beavers have to repair it. They often have to make the dam higher and wider to hold the water which backs up in the pond.

3. Why the Beavers Build Dams

The beavers do all this work in order to have a deep pond. Do you know why they want this pond? They need it for protection. When they splash into it, they are safe from all their enemies.

Beavers also use the pond as a place in which to keep their food. The bark of all the branches and logs which they cut is their food. They pile these logs in the pond and eat the bark all winter.

The pond is useful, too, for floating these logs to the lodge. The real home of the beaver is the lodge. It is built in the deep part of the pond.

4. How Beavers Build Their Lodges

Beavers must have homes just as bees, ants, birds, and people do.

Some beavers build their homes in the bank near the pond. Others build them partly in the water and partly on the bank. Most beavers build

**Why doesn't the beaver build its nest
on dry land instead of in the water?**

their stick lodges right out in the pond. These are
called island lodges. Can you see why they are?

The lodge is built of sticks and mud just as
the dam is. First a firm bottom must be made.
Then the sticks and mud are piled higher and
higher. The lodge is partly above the water.
These lodges are of different sizes. Some are only
five to six feet high. Others are ten to twelve
feet high.

You will wonder how the beavers get into their

lodges. There is no door on the top. They do not want their enemies to visit them. The door is always under water. It must be near enough to the bottom of the pond so that it won't freeze shut in winter.

How about the inside of the lodge? Does it have rooms like an ant hill? The lodge has really two stories, an upstairs and a downstairs. The upstairs is the living room. Here the beavers eat, sleep, and hide. This floor is above the water. It is dry upstairs. The downstairs is the landing room. The beavers wait here until most of the water has dripped off from them. That keeps the living room dry. How high do you think the downstairs room is? It is only about eighteen inches. How high is the downstairs part in your house?

5. How Beavers Build Canals

There is another job which beavers do that will interest you. They not only build dams and lodges; they also build canals, or ditches. These canals join ponds with other streams or ponds. They are useful for floating the logs to the lodges. They are also a protection to the beavers in case an enemy comes suddenly upon them.

What use do the beavers
make of canals like these?

Just as men have built canals to carry goods, so the beavers have built their canals to carry their goods. Some of the canals are only a few feet long. Others are several hundred feet long.

6. The Beaver Family

Beavers are social just as ants and bees and people are social. They live and work together in a family. Each one helps the others.

There is no queen or king in a beaver family. The father and mother beavers live together with their families in much the same way your fathers and mothers live with you. The fathers do the tree cutting and hauling. The mothers tend their families and help build the dams and lodges.

Most families have three to six babies. Some families have as many as eight. The beavers are very careful mothers. They do not let their babies leave the pond until they are almost a year old. They stay in the pond where they are safe until they are old enough to protect themselves.

Should an enemy come, the father or mother beaver gives the water a slap with its broad tail. What a noise it makes! That means: "Swim to your lodge. An enemy is near!" No more will be seen of the beavers for some time.

It is a good thing that mother beavers watch their babies so carefully. Beavers have so many enemies that it would not be safe for a baby beaver to go far away.

Men have always trapped the beavers. They want their fine, thick, brown coats of fur to use for coats, hats, and muffs.

Even the Indians trapped the beavers. They used the skins as we use money. They traded beaver skins for the other things they needed.

Things to Think About

1. What do beavers gain by living together?

2. How are beavers useful to man?

3. Why are beavers sometimes called engineers, carpenters, and lumbermen?

4. What three remarkable things do beavers build?

5. In what ways are the beavers being protected by our government?

Things to Do

1. Put this list of names of animals in two groups — mammals and insects:

grasshopper	horse
cow	mosquito
fly	butterfly
elephant	dog
sheep	beetle

2. Write a story telling how Paddy the Beaver lives. Draw pictures for your story.

Problem 2 · Animals That Live Together at Times

1. Animals That Live Together for Protection

Some animals are not so social as the ones about which you have been reading. A good many animals live together for only part of the year. The rest of the time they live alone. Can you think of any reasons why animals might live together only at certain times? This story about animals will help you find out why some animals want to live together at times.

Several years ago Theodore Roosevelt went to Africa to hunt. He was not hunting small game. He was not hunting tame animals. He was hunting large, wild animals like lions and tigers. Did he go alone? No, he wanted the help and protection of other good hunters. He took a party with him. They gave him added protection on his dangerous trip.

So it is with many animals. They are often better able to protect themselves when banded together.

When the white men first went to the western

© J. E. Haynes

Would this herd of buffalo need to fear the wolves?

part of our country, they found great herds of buffaloes eating on the western plains. These animals lived in herds because they could protect themselves from their enemies, the wolves, by living this way. No one buffalo was able to fight off a pack of wolves. But by helping each other they could drive the wolves away.

Make a list of five other animals that live together for protection.

2. Animals That Live Together While Migrating

My, what a noise and clatter! What can it be? You run to the door and see hundreds of noisy grackles circling in the air. Soon they light upon the meadow, and all is quiet for a time. In a moment the noise begins all over again. The birds are flying again, and the air is black with them. Soon they are only black specks far away.

"I saw a flock of geese fly north today," my father used to say. " Warm weather will be here soon." We have weather bureaus now which tell us what kind of weather is coming. In olden days people had strange kinds of weather men. Birds were one kind of weather man. Their coming meant that the spring was near. Their going told people that winter was coming.

This movement from place to place is called migration. Scientists used to think that birds migrated to get more food and to have a comfortable place in which to spend the winter months. Since many birds migrate even though they have plenty of food and a comfortable place to live, scientists are puzzled about the migration of these feathered friends.

©A. M. N. H.

The geese are flying north again. Spring must be on its way

During the time of migration birds live in flocks. They flock together and seem to follow a leader over the bird roadways of the air.

Birds had air roadways long before man made airplanes. They choose air routes and follow them just as Lindbergh and other fliers have laid out the best air routes for airplanes.

Birds are not the only animals that migrate. The reindeer of the north migrate in herds to search for food. The salmon migrate up streams in order to lay their eggs. Whales, seals, and sea lions migrate, too. They travel far to find just the right spot in which to raise their families.

3. Animals That Live Together to Raise a Family

Have you ever watched the birds in the springtime? Each one is trying to find a mate. That is why they have on their finest clothes. By fall all their bright coats will be quite dull. But when they are looking for mates they must look their best.

Soon you will see a pair of robins here, and a pair of wrens there. They have decided to build themselves a cozy home. How hard they work! A bit of straw, a piece of string, some grass, some mud, and much hard work are needed before the nest is ready.

After the eggs are laid the mother bird sits on them to keep them warm. The father takes good care of his mate. He brings her worms and seeds to eat. He stays near her to help her protect the eggs.

When you go to the zoo or to a circus, you see many animals that do not live in our country.

Do you think this lion makes a good mother?

Many of these animals are large and fierce. They do not need to live together for protection. They can protect themselves. The lions, the tigers, the jaguars, and the pumas live by themselves most of the time. When they want to have families they live together. After the babies arrive the mother takes most of the care of them. You might call the father lazy. He leaves all the care of the children to the mother. It really isn't always a hard job, as most of the animal babies grow up very fast. They are soon able to look after themselves. Then they leave their mother

Indians driving frightened animals into a
pound. They needed the animals for food

and go off alone. Think how long it takes you to
be able to take care of yourself. How long would
it take a baby lion or bear?

4. Animals That Unite for Hunting

Long years ago the Indians used to hunt in
large groups. They would first build a "pound."
A pound was really a large trap. It was like a big
round fence with gates which could be closed.

After the pound was built the Indians would

Pelicans unite to catch fish

start hunting. They would make a huge circle and travel for miles toward the pound. While walking they beat upon their drums. The noise frightened the deer and other wild animals. They would run to get away from it. Soon they would be caught in the pound.

Even today in Africa there are some tribes of natives who still use this old way of hunting. They beat the bushes with sticks and drive the animals before them into a pound. In this way they catch their food easily.

Many animals unite to get food, too. They are better able to catch their prey that way. Wolves hunt in packs. They can attack and kill animals much larger than themselves. Living in packs helps them to get more food.

Pelicans unite to catch the fish which they eat. Storks unite to catch grasshoppers.

5. Why Some Animals Do Not Live Together

When you go for a walk with other children, is there likely to be a lot of noise? Do you sometimes enjoy being all alone?

When many animals get together, there may also be a great deal of noise. Some animals would rather live by themselves.

A family of coyotes are pretty noisy. Their cries are often heard by the hunters. If the coyotes lived alone, they would be less likely to be found by their enemies.

Many animals have a strange odor. One animal alone would not be so likely to be discovered as a colony would. The odor would be much stronger when many were together, and enemies would find them more easily.

If there is but little food it might be better for an animal to hunt alone. Then whatever he caught would be all his. If he were hunting with others, he would have to share whatever he got.

Sometimes many animals have had trouble in finding food, because there were so many that liked the same kind. Farmers know that if they put too many cattle in a field, there will not be enough grass to go around. Of course the wild animals have no kind-hearted farmers to look after them.

 Things to Think About

1. Why do animals live together?

2. What animals unite for migration?

3. What animals unite for protection?

4. What animals unite for raising families?

 *Things to Do*

1. Watch the birds that live near your home. Notice them building their nests. Note when they begin to gather in flocks and migrate. Some birds are known to return year after year to the same nesting place.

2. Keep a record of the dates when you see your first robin, bluebird, wren, song sparrow, and other birds. Keep this record and check it with next year's record. Birds return at about the same date each year.

UNIT VII
The Value of Animals and Plants

Have you ever stopped to think why no one lived on the earth when it was young? It is impossible for any person to live without the help of plants and other animals. At first the earth had neither of these two necessary things. Until plants began to grow, no animals could live, because there was no food for them to eat. Plants and animals are of great value to us. Let us find out some of the many ways in which they help us.

Problem 1 · What Animals Do for Us

Did you ever stop to think about what animals do for us? They are quite as useful to us as plants are. This story will tell you some of the ways in which animals help man.

1. Animals Eat Insects

Some scientists tell us that if all our birds were to be destroyed, it would be only about seven years before man and other animals of the earth would begin to starve. Seven years is only a short time.

Birds help us because they kill insects. Without them the earth would soon be full of buzzing, crawling, creeping, hopping, flying insects. These insects, feeding upon plants, would soon destroy them all. They would strip the trees, plants, and bushes of their leaves and seeds. Almost every ear of corn, every kernel of wheat, would be eaten by this army of insects.

There really would be an army of them, too. Without birds to destroy them there would be little chance for plants or animals upon the earth.

If you have ever been camping near a lake in

c

the summer time, you know how many mosquitoes there are to bite you. They never leave you alone. Imagine how many, many more there would be if thousands of them were not gobbled up daily by birds.

There are the garden pests which the birds destroy. The cutworms, the white grubs, the grasshoppers, and the beetles which destroy plants are all favorite food for many of our common birds. Even the crow, which many farmers shoot, does more good than harm. It eats corn, to be sure, but it also destroys thousands of harmful insects which are the farmer's enemies.

Think of all the other birds that help us. Robins, grosbeaks, song sparrows, tree sparrows, meadow larks, wrens, and martins are all busy keeping down our insect pests.

Birds not only eat insects. Some of them eat seeds. Many of these are weed seeds which farmers do not want. Of course birds eat seeds of the grain which the farmer wants, too. But the good they do by eating weed seeds makes up for some of the grain seeds. If you are wise, you will protect the birds.

The homely garden toad is a helper of ours, too. It is an insect eater. While we are asleep the toad

Martin

Wren

Meadow Lark

Grosbeak

Song Sparrow

Robin

From a painting by Harold M. Sichel

These birds are our friends

hops about gobbling up the many night-flying insects.

While we are speaking of insect eaters, we must not forget the snakes. They are very helpful. They also eat mice which are found in the fields eating more than their share of the farmer's grain.

2. Animals Give Us Food

Of course we must not forget that many animals provide us with food. Can you remember the last time you had a piece of delicious chicken or a slice of roast lamb? Most of us eat some meat every day.

Besides giving us meat, cows give us milk and cream. We use the milk for part of our food. Mother makes or buys butter which has been made from cream.

You must also remember that the hens furnish the eggs which you eat for breakfast or luncheon.

3. Animals Give Us Clothing

Long ago people learned to use the skins of animals for clothing. By cleaning them carefully and soaking them, they softened the skins. People found the skins of many animals warm and comfortable.

What heavy warm clothing the Eskimos wear!

Have you ever seen an Eskimo suit? Eskimos use the skins of polar bears and other animals to make their warm suits. Each suit has two skins. The under one has the fur on the inside. The top one has the fur on the outside. Two layers of fur keep the Eskimos warm enough in their cold north-land.

How lovely the Indian suits are! They are almost always made from the skins of deer. Some of them have beadwork on them. Others are painted in gay colors. Some Indians use animal skins for their houses too.

You wear animal skins. What are your gloves made of? Yes, and your shoes? Have you a fur collar on your winter coat? All of you have sweaters. They are made from the warm wool which grows on the sheep's back. Your heavy winter clothes are probably made of wool, too.

 Things to Think About

1. What other animals help man besides those you have read about in this story?

2. In how many ways do animals help man?

3. Birds are often called "Balancers of Nature." How do you think they got that name?

4. What harmful insects do birds destroy?

 *Things to Do*

1. Watch a robin on your front lawn. Notice what it eats.

2. Make a list of all the birds which live near you that are helpful to man.

3. If you have a garden, be sure to find a toad to help you garden. Watch him each day, and you will see that he is a good helper.

4. Since animals are so valuable to us we should do all we can to protect them. Many of you probably have a rabbit, bird, cat, or dog for a pet. Do you take good care of it? Here are some important things to remember in caring for your pet:

> *a.* Keep the cage, or yard, in which your pet lives, clean.
>
> *b.* Provide your pet with the right amount of food and water, as well as a proper place to exercise and rest.
>
> *c.* Many domestic animals have pests which bother them. By keeping the animals clean you can help them to be free from these pests.
>
> *d.* Do not handle your pets too much.

5. The next time you go to a circus, or to the zoo, or to a farm, notice the way the animals are cared for. Notice how they are fed and watered. See how clean their homes are kept.

Problem 2 · What Plants Do for Us

1. Plants Give Us Food

How queer the earth must have looked when it was young! Remember, it had no plants. It had only rocks and water and air. No people lived upon the earth then. People can't live on just rocks and water and air. They need food, clothing, and houses in which to live.

I'm afraid you would say, "No, thank you," if mother passed you a piece of rock for your supper. Even King Midas did not like gold for food.

There were no animals upon the earth until there were plants. So your mother couldn't give you a piece of meat instead of rock.

All animals depend upon plants for food. Of course some animals eat other animals. But the animals which were eaten had to get their food from plants.

The story may go like this.

> A tiger ate a fox;
> The fox ate a cat;
> The cat lapped the milk
> Of the old Jersey cow;
>
> *But the cow ate grass.*

An eagle caught a hawk;
The hawk caught a weasel;
The weasel dined upon a chick
  Which lived in a coop;

But the chick ate corn.

All animals depend upon plants for food. Without plants this earth would still be only land, air, and water. What a bare place, indeed!

Make a list of all the foods you eat which are plants. All the fruits you eat are plants. All the vegetables you eat are plants. All the meat you eat comes from animals which eat plants. The cereal you had for breakfast was made from plants. You would have no delicious nuts, raisins, dates, peaches, or candy if it were not for plants. Should you like to live without these good things to eat? Could you live without some of them?

2. Plants Give Us Clothes

What a nice warm suit you are wearing! Where did it come from? Of what is it made?

Your coat and trousers are made of wool. Somewhere miles away from you a sheep was robbed of her soft, warm coat in order that you might have that suit.

And where did the sheep get it? She ate upon the rocky hillsides, nibbling the grass and bushes that grow there. She ate plants in order to grow that wool of which your suit was made.

"Did my blouse come from a plant, too?" you ask.

Yes, indeed. In the sunny south-land, on a very large farm, grew the cotton of which your blouse is made. All summer long the cotton plant was busy storing the soft white stuff in its seed pod, or boll. Then one day when the boll was full and ripe enough it burst. It was picked and sent to the factory which made your blouse.

"What about my tie?"

It is silk. The thread which made it had a long ocean journey. It came from Japan. A tiny silk-worm spun it for a soft cocoon cradle in which to go to sleep. But man did not let him sleep in it long. It was too valuable for that. It was spun on a spool, and later it was woven into a tie.

Your leather belt and shoes were once the skin of some animal. But remember that all animals depend upon plants for food. Should you have had your shoes and belt without plants?

Can you think of anything which you wear that was not made from plants or animals?

When you wear linen knickers, you are really wearing the stalks of a plant called flax.

When you dress up in your Indian suit, you are wearing a plant called hemp.

Even your jumping rope and the rope you use for your swing are made from plants. They are made from hemp, too.

3. Plants Give Us Shelter

Is your house made of wood, or stone, or brick, or concrete? If it is made of wood, then it is really made from a plant. Trees are very large plants.

What about your furniture? I imagine most of it is made of wood. How many things in your house are made of wood?

Some Japanese houses have paper sides with bamboo frames. "Surely," you will say, "these are not made from plants." You are wrong. Paper is made from wood, straw, or rags. All these are parts of plants.

When you go for a camping trip the tent which you sleep in is made from plants.

Of course there are other materials used in building. Wood is only one, but it is an important one.

What four useful things are made from these plants?

4. Plants Help us to have Oxygen

Plants help to make the air fit for us to breathe.
They use carbon dioxide in their food factory and
give back oxygen to the air. If it weren't for
plants we should have much less oxygen to breathe.

5. Plants Are Used As Medicine

When I was a little girl, my grandmother used
to give me homemade medicine. She was no doctor, but she knew how to make medicine for us.
Strange to say, it was usually very good, too. We
liked to take it.

She gathered catnip for catnip tea. She gathered pokeweed root for salve. Whenever we got
burned she would make us well by rubbing on
pokeweed-root salve.

If we caught cold she gave us cough medicine
which she had made from vinegar, butter, and
sugar. Of course the vinegar was made from the
juice of apples which she had pressed herself.

You must have read many stories about the
"wise woman of the woods" and the Indian "medicine men." They both used plants called herbs
in making their medicines.

A Navaho Indian medicine man. He is mixing a potion to use to drive evil spirits away

The people thought these witches and medicine men were very, very wise. Today, however, we think they were not so wise as they were clever. Some of the things the medicine men made were good cures for illness. That is how people came to believe they were magic. You and I know, of course, that our doctors would be much more able to cure us than the medicine men of earlier days. Mother would not think of calling an Indian medicine man if you were ill. She would call a doctor.

6. Plants Are Used for Coloring

In one museum which I visit often there is a case full of blankets which were made by Navaho Indians. I like to look at them because of their lovely bright colors.

Near the blankets there is some pottery. It was made by the Zuñi Indians, who are neighbors of the Navahos. How lovely their designs are!

The colors used in dyeing the wool for the blankets and in painting the designs on the pottery were made from the berries and the roots of plants. What a lot of work it was to prepare these colors!

Most people today use factory-made dyes for coloring. Many Indians use them, too. But they never get such lovely, clear color as they do when they make their own.

7. Plants Are Used to Add Beauty

Mother and father built a new house. It was made of beautiful material. It was set 'way back upon a large lot. It was painted white. But there was something wrong with it. It did not really look right. There was something missing.

Of course it did not take them long to discover what the trouble was. There was no lovely green

Compare this picture with the one below. What is the difference?

Should you like to live here?

lawn; there were no shrubs, no shade trees, no flowers about. How bare it looked!

They set to work to make their new house look more homelike. Shrubs were planted. Flower beds were made. The yard was planted with grass seed.

What a difference there was a year from then! The lawn was a bright green. The shrubs were white and green. The yellow daffodils seemed to be trying to outdo the bed of yellow and red tulips.

"Plants make all the difference in the world," they said.

Why does mother buy flowers for the table? Why does your teacher like plants in your schoolroom?

I wonder if you have ever gone walking in the woods in the spring of the year when the wild flowers were in full bloom? Have you seen the velvet carpet which purple violets spread along the banks of a tiny stream? Have you waded in the marshland in search of the dainty pink lady-slipper orchid? Have you seen the flower of the pitcher plant standing straight and tall? Then, there are the yellow buttercup, the drooping trillium, the adders'-tongue, and the graceful columbine for you to feast your eyes upon.

These and many other wild flowers used to grow in great numbers in the woodlands. In some places there are still plenty to be found, but many places which used to be lovely with wild flowers are now without them.

Thoughtless boys and girls as well as grown-ups have picked so many of the flowers that few were left to go to seed. Unless all of us join in protecting our wild flowers, many of the very loveliest kinds are soon going to disappear. You may find out the names of the wild flowers you should be especially careful to protect by writing to the Wild Flower Preservation Society, Washington, D. C. You may also find out the names of ones you may pick. When you pick your bouquet, do not pick a great many. A few flowers in a vase are usually much lovelier than a crowded bouquet.

8. Plants Help Hold the Soil to the Earth

A long line of camels was journeying across the desert. Soon the men that were riding them became worried. A sand storm was coming. The camels and men put their heads close to the ground. That was their way of protecting themselves during the storm.

c

During the sand storms in the deserts caravans are halted. Why are the camels and men in this position?

Sand storms are common in deserts. There is nothing to hold the sand to the earth. It blows about with the gentlest wind.

We have already read about tombs which the kings of Egypt built long ago, and which have been partly buried by the sand which has blown across the desert.

The roots of plants keep the soil from blowing about. Did you ever see a sand storm in a grass meadow?

Evergreen trees are often planted along the
banks of reservoirs. Do you know why?

9. How Plants Keep Moisture in the Earth

Large cities use a great deal of water. Most
cities have large reservoirs in which to store their
water. All along the banks of the reservoir they
plant evergreen trees. You may think they do it
just to make the reservoir more beautiful.

They have another reason for wanting these trees
there. The trees keep the rain from running away
as it falls. They keep the moisture in the ground.

Did you ever notice how very wet the ground is
in the middle of a deep, deep forest? That is be-

cause the roots keep the rain from running away. The leaves also keep the sun from shining upon the ground. Not very much of the water can evaporate back into the air.

10. How Plants Protect Themselves

My! My! how very important plants are anyway. They give us our food, our clothing, and some of our shelter. They make the earth beautiful. They give off oxygen for us to breathe. They keep the soil from blowing about.

Since plants are so important to us, what a good thing it is that they can protect themselves from their enemies. Some plants have thorns, to keep away animals that would eat them. The raspberry bushes, the rosebushes, and the thistles all have thorns.

Other plants are protected because they have an unpleasant odor or taste. The smartweed and sorrel are these kinds of plants.

In wet weather the bark prevents the rain from injuring the plants, and in hot weather the bark keeps the sap in the trees from evaporating. Before cold weather arrives many trees drop their leaves. This is a great protection against the heavy falls of snow, which might break the branches.

Things to Think About

1. Why is all life dependent upon plants?

2. In what different ways do plants help us in our everyday living?

3. How did the Egyptians of long ago use plants?

4. What did the Indians use plants for?

5. Plants help to keep us healthy in the following ways:

  a. They are part of the food which we eat.

  b. They use the carbon dioxide which we breathe out.

  c. They give off oxygen which we need in order to live.

  d. They furnish some of the material we use for clothing.

Things to Do

1. Make a list of all the articles of clothing you are wearing which were made from parts of plants.

2. Make a list of all the plants used in your school room. Don't forget your books, tablets, and pencils.

3. Try to make some dye out of berries and roots. Dye some cloth in it. If you need clothing dyed for a play costume, you may want to use some of your home-made dye for it.

4. What can you do to make your school room more beautiful?

5. Write to the Wild Flower Preservation Society, Washington, D. C., to find out what wild flowers you may pick and what ones you should protect.

UNIT VIII

Plants

PLANTS

Gardening is a lot of fun. You may want to make a garden this spring. If you want to be a good gardener, you will need to know how to prepare the ground and plant the seeds. The next chapter will tell you a great many things about how to do this.

Most of the plants you see growing in gardens start from tiny seeds. Some plants, like mushrooms and puffballs, do not grow from seeds but start in quite another way, which is explained in Problem 2, Plants Without Seeds.

Problem 1 · How to Make a Garden

What a lovely garden! Jack and Dorothy made it. They have watched it grow from the very first. How happy they were when the first tiny green shoots peeped through the ground!

Day after day they watched their garden grow. They could hardly wait for the first blossoms to come. The sweet alyssum blossomed first. Then the beautiful yellow daisies burst into bloom. It was not long before the garden was full of color. Red nasturtiums, blue phlox, purple bachelor's-buttons, yellow and purple pansies, together made a beautiful sight.

No wonder the children are proud of it! They have good reason to be. It took them many hours of real work to make this garden.

Perhaps you may want to have a garden all your own this year. If you could make one as nice as the one Jack and Dorothy made, it would be worth trying.

Jack and Dorothy were good gardeners. They did all the things which they had learned to do for garden making. Perhaps you would like to prepare your garden as they did. Here are the things they did. It was hard work, but they liked doing it. They really wanted to have a beautiful garden.

1. Choosing a Garden Spot

First of all Jack and Dorothy had to choose a place for their garden. They did not want to have a large one, because it was their first year to garden.

Of course they had to be sure to pick out a sunny spot. They could not make it behind the garage, because there was no sun there all the morning. They could not make it near the big maple tree, because the sun could not get at it there.

Father gave them just the right spot. It was at the end of the lot. It had the sun nearly all day. Father said, "Here's just the place for my two gardeners to go to work."

He had another reason for choosing this spot. He chose it because the soil there was the right kind for a good garden. You can't make your garden in just any old place. You must be sure that the place you pick has the right kind of soil. Soil furnishes much of the materials which the plant uses for food.

2. Kinds of Soil

The children's father explained to them about soil. He showed them how to test their soil to see just what kind it was.

These are the materials they found in soil.

sand		loam
	silt	
clay		gravel

Sand, clay, silt, and gravel are formed from rocks. Do you remember that wind and water are at work all the time wearing rocks away? They have been wearing them away for thousands of years. That is how soil has formed.

The very large, coarse material in soil is gravel. It is used in building roads. Gravel is very poor soil for plants.

Sand is finer than gravel. It blows about more easily. It is very good for some plants. Beans and rye grow well in sandy soil.

Of course you know what clay looks like. When dry it is like a very fine powder. When wet it sticks to your shoes like glue.

Silt is very fine rock. It is so fine that it is carried along in streams of water. Sometimes it gives the water a yellow color.

These children are testing soil to
find out what materials are in it

Loam is a mixture of clay and sand. It also
has decayed vegetable matter in it. When leaves,
stems, and roots of plants decay, they mix with the
soil, forming loam. This kind of soil is best for
gardening.

3. Testing the Soil

Jack and Dorothy tested their soil. They put a
handful of it into a fruit jar. They filled the jar
about half full of water and let it stand for a day.

When they looked at it, they found that the soil

had formed in layers. There was a little heavy gravel, which fell to the bottom. There was a thick layer of sand next. On top of it was a thinner layer of clay. At the very top was a thin layer of silt.

All the children had to do was to look for the thickest layers. They were sand and clay. They knew that their garden was made up mostly of these two soils. It was loam.

Father told them that their land needed some fertilizer. Fertilizer makes plants grow better. He said that manure would be best for that kind of soil. He also told them that the soil was sour, and sour soil is not good for plants to grow in. He told them to mix a little lime with the soil to keep it from being sour.

4. Raking the Space for the Garden

On the very first warm, sunny, spring day Jack and Dorothy got busy. They took their rake and spade and went to work.

All the rubbish was raked into a pile and burned. What a cheerful, blazing fire it made! They left the ashes on the garden to help fertilize it.

Perhaps you do not know what "fertilize" means. Jack and Dorothy learned that fertile soil has plenty of material in it for plants to make food from. Manure and other fertilizing materials have the materials which plants use. When you put any of those things on the garden, you fertilize it.

5. Spading the Garden

The children had to have some help in getting the garden ready, and their father was glad to give them a little boost. He spaded it for them. Gardens need to be spaded deeply. That brings the soil which has been down underneath up to the surface.

It didn't seem hard to do. The children thought they would like to try. They found that a spade full of soil was very heavy.

"What does spading do to the soil?" asked Dorothy.

"You wouldn't have much of a garden if you didn't spade it," father answered. "Spading breaks and loosens the soil, so that the tiny roots of the plants can grow down into it. Roots need to be able to grow in order to get food for the plants."

After the garden was well spaded, the children smoothed it off by raking it. Then they were ready to plant the seeds.

6. Planting the Garden

That was a great day. They had waited to be sure that there would be no more frosts. It seemed to them that their father would never find a day which he thought was warm enough.

"Today's the day," he said at last.

They took the seeds which they had chosen and set to work. They had made a plan on paper of just how the garden was to look.

The sweet alyssum was to be planted around the edge to form a lovely border for the bed.

The pansies were to be planted next. Then the nasturtiums. Then the bachelor's-buttons. Last of all, the marigolds and cosmos.

The children dug shallow rows about an inch deep. What fun it was to drop the seeds and lose them in the soil! They covered the rows with soil, using their hands. If they had covered them too deeply, it would have taken a long time for the plants to peep through the ground.

How they watched! One day passed. Two

days, three days, four days, five, six days. It seemed that they would never see the tiny plants.

They watered the garden every evening. Plants need water in order to grow. They drink the water through their drinking cups. Their roots are their drinking cups. That is how they get the material they need for making their food. It is in the water.

7. How the Children Helped the Plants

Everything that the children did to their garden helped the plants get water. They kept the weeds out so that they would not rob the plants of water.

Jack and Dorothy cultivated the garden often. They had a hand cultivator which they pushed along between the rows of plants. Sometimes the plants were so close together that they cultivated the soil with a hoe. This helped the plants keep the water. It kept the soil from making a hard crust on the top.

Let a piece of ground get hard on top, and see what it does. Great cracks will form in it. When the sun is hot, the water in the soil evaporates through these cracks.

Jack and Dorothy did not let their garden get hard on top. They cultivated it and kept a soft.

These children are proud of their flowers.
They enjoy working in their garden

dry mulch on top. A mulch is a loose, soft mixture of soil. Then the water could not evaporate so fast. It stayed in the ground for the plants to use.

This little garden blossomed all summer. The more the children picked the flowers the more they blossomed.

They decided to have a bigger garden the next year. Do you think it would be as lovely as this one?

 ### *Things to Think About*

1. When you make a garden, what things do you need to remember?

2. Plan your garden so that you have flowers blooming at different times during the summer. What flowers would you choose for such a garden?

3. Why is it important to test your soil before planting your garden?

4. Why is water necessary to plants?

 ### *Things to Do*

1. Perhaps you cannot have an outdoor garden. Why not make a window-box garden? Get good fertile soil for it. Nail it to a window that gets the sun. A south or west window is best. Keep it well watered and cultivated. A fork makes a good cultivator for a window-box garden.

When the garden blossoms, keep watch for visitors. A tiny humming bird may pay the box a visit. See what flowers it seems to like best. Watch for bees, too. They are sure to come often.

2. You may want to experiment with soil. Put some sand in one glass jar, loam in another, and clay in another. Plant the same kind of seeds in each jar. Watch them every day. See what happens.

Which is the best soil for the plant that you chose to grow? Do the roots all grow alike? There are two things which plants need in order to grow. What are they?

3. Plant a sweet potato in water in a glass jar. Watch it sprout and grow. The vine will make a pretty green spot in your room.

4. Plan a vegetable garden. Be sure to plant foods which are good for you. Green leafy vegetables such as cabbage, spinach, and lettuce are fine food to eat. Plan to include peas, beans, and tomatoes too.

Problem 2 · Plants Without Seeds

Have you ever wondered

Why a puffball makes a cloud of dust when you step upon it?

Why old bread gets moldy in damp, warm weather?

What mushrooms really are?

Why your mother irons her clothes within a day or two after sprinkling them?

Why your mother bothers to dry and clean all your winter clothing before she puts it away for the summer?

The plants which you have been reading about all grew from seeds. These seeds were planted in the garden. Soon tiny plants appeared where the seeds had been planted. Inside every seed was a tiny baby plant. This baby plant started growing. It sent roots down into the ground to get food. It sent stems and leaves up through the ground into the air to get the sunshine.

Seeds do not all look alike. They may be nuts, like the acorn or chestnut. They may be burs, like those of the burdock or thistle. They may have wings which carry them miles in the wind.

When these nuts and burs are planted, new plants grow from them.

There are some plants that do not grow from

These are the puffballs you have been reading about. What would happen if you stepped on them?

seeds. You have seen some of these plants many times. Mushrooms do not grow from seeds. Puffballs do not grow from seeds. They grow from tiny spores which act something like seeds. One of these spores is so small that you and I cannot see it except under a microscope. Puffballs and mushrooms are called fungi.

When you have been walking in the woods you must have seen puffballs. It is fun to step on them. Just burst the brown skin, and what a cloud of brown dust flies into the air! This dust has many spores in it. Each of these spores can form a new puffball if it finds a good place in which to grow.

There are spores in the air all the time. When

it is warm and damp they rest upon animal or plant life and begin to grow.

When you were a tiny baby your mother had to feed you. You could not get your own food. Most plants have to make their own food. They take material from the ground and air and with the sun's help make the food which they need.

Fungi cannot make their own food. They have to get their food from other plants or from animals. They use food which has already been made. That is why fungi can grow in dark, damp places. They do not need help from the sun, because they steal food which has already been made.

Perhaps you have a dog that likes to play with old leather shoes. Almost every dog likes to drag an old shoe about and play with it. Of course the leather gets wet from being carried in the dog's mouth. When it is still damp, the dog may hide it in a dark corner. If it is left there a few days, it will be covered with mold.

Mold grows from spores. The tiny spores in the air lodged upon the damp shoe and started growing. They got their food from the leather.

Years and years ago mold used to be a mystery to people. It would form upon their bread. They wondered where the queer green stuff came from.

When they put their bread away it would be fresh. But when they were ready to eat it a few days later, it might be covered with mold. They did not know that the air is full of spores which grow rapidly in warm, damp places.

How should you like to grow a mold garden for yourself? It is one of the easiest gardens to grow. Here is one way to grow a mold garden.

Moisten a piece of bread. Put it in a jelly glass. Put the cover on the glass. Find a warm, dark spot in your room and put the glass there. In a few days you will have a mold garden.

Some people have tried to grow a mold garden in another way. Try it and see what happens.

Place a piece of dry bread in a jelly glass. Cover the glass and place it in a cool dry place. Leave it several days. See if a mold garden grows for you.

Probably you think that your mother keeps the clothes in the clothes closet dry because she is afraid of moths. That is one reason why she wants them clean and dry. But she also wants to be sure that the clothes do not mold.

When clothes are damp they are likely to become covered with a green mold called mildew. If your mother did not iron the clothes within a day or two after sprinkling them, they would be likely to mildew. Just try it. Dampen an old towel and roll it up. Put it in a warm place. Look at it three or four days later. You will see why your mother wants to have the clothes ironed soon after they are sprinkled.

When I was a little girl I used to like to go to my grandmother's house to visit. I thought she was about the best cook I ever knew. She used to bake the most delicious cakes, pies, doughnuts, and tarts that anyone ever ate. She baked home-made bread too. She would take loaf after loaf from the big, hot oven.

Grandmother did not make bread just as bakers do today. They make bread by using yeast cakes. Grandmother never heard of a yeast cake. There were no yeast cakes made in her day. She made her own yeast. She used potato water and sugar to make it. The spores in the air grew in the potato water and made yeast.

This yeast is a fungus, too. It is not just like mold, however. When you put it into bread dough it feeds upon the sugar in the dough. While doing so it changes the sugar to carbon dioxide and alcohol. The carbon dioxide bubbles try to get out. As they push their way up through the dough they make holes, or pores, in it. That is what makes bread rise, or get light, as my grandmother used to say. Meanwhile the alcohol gets so hot it turns to vapor and evaporates into the air.

How did this mushroom happen to grow here?

On the first warm, wet days of spring, mushrooms will start growing. Mushrooms are fungi. They get their food from other things because they cannot make their own food. Do not gather these fungi. They may be poisonous.

Mushrooms which we eat are grown on mushroom farms in damp soil or sawdust. The buildings in which these mushrooms are grown are kept very warm.

Farmers would be glad if they could get rid of some of the spores that are in the air. Spores often ruin the farmers' crops. Some spores lodge on ears of corn and cause a disease called smut. Other spores lodge upon kernels of wheat and cause a disease called rust. Still other spores lodge upon fruit and cause a disease called blight. When these things happen the farmers lose money.

One kind of spore which is in the air helps to make cheese. This cheese is made of goat's milk and is then placed in musty, damp caves in France. The spores in these caves form a mold upon the cheese. If you have ever eaten Roquefort cheese you have eaten mold. The greenish part of the cheese is mold.

Spores have caused this ear of corn to be diseased. The disease is called smut

These tiny spores are great travelers. They are very, very light. So many of them are present in the air that they fly about almost everywhere. Aviators have found spores as high as two miles in the air. They caught them on moist plates of glass. It is no wonder that we find mold and mildew so often.

Things to Think About

1. What are fungi?

2. In what ways are fungi different from ordinary garden plants?

3. What other fungi do you know besides the ones you have just read about?

4. The air is full of bacteria. Some of these bacteria are helpful and some of them are harmful. Since we cannot see the bacteria in the air, we have to be very careful not to get the harmful ones in our bodies — that is, not to get any more of them in than we can help. Putting our hands in our mouths, biting our finger nails, or eating fruit that has not been washed are all very bad habits because it is in these ways that a great many bacteria get into our bodies. Be sure to wash your hands with soap and warm water before handling your food.

Things to Do

1. Grow a mold garden on bread.

2. Grow a mold garden on leather.

3. Grow a mold garden in a book. Be sure to use a magazine or book which is of no use. Dampen it and put it away in a warm place. You will soon have a fine mold garden. Look at the mold through a magnifying glass.

4. Try to make some yeast like that your grandmother used to make.

UNIT IX

Two Forces Which Man Has Put to Work

1. How Electricity Works
2. Why Steam Has Power

Have you ever wondered:

> Why a doorbell rings when you press a button?
>
> How a flash light works?
>
> How steam makes a giant locomotive pull a heavy load of cars along a shiny track?

All these things happen because man has harnessed two great forces of nature and made them work for him. They are electricity and steam. The next two stories will tell you just how man has put these two great forces to work.

Problem I · How Electricity Works

You must know something about electricity.
When you push a button, your room becomes
lighted. When your mother washes, she lets electricity run the washing machine. When you want
to hear some music, you turn on the electric radio.
If some one needs a doctor, you call him on the
telephone. In what other ways does electricity
help people?

It is hard to think just what we should do without electricity. We should have to use candles,
oil, or gas for our lights. We should have to sweep
with a broom. We should ride in carriages drawn
by horses instead of in automobiles. We should
not be able to telephone or telegraph. Our newspapers would have to be printed by hand. What
a change there would be in our living if electricity
were not our slave!

1. What Dry Cells Are

Dry cells are good to work with. They will not
give you a shock. You need never be afraid of
touching them or the wires leading from them.
They cannot hurt you.

Here are some things which run by electricity. Can you think of other things which run by electricity?

A dry cell is not really dry. If you cut one apart you will find that it has a moist black paste inside it.

People call these cells dry because they do not let any of the black paste spill out. They are dry on the outside.

2. Working With Dry Cells

You may want to know how to work with electricity. You do not need to wait until you are grown up. Suppose we work a little with it right

These children have all the things you will need for wiring your bell. See if you can name all the things they are using

now. Let's wire a bell. You may use the bell for a doorbell. Your mother may use it to call you when she needs you. Your teacher might use it to call you in from recess.

You need only a few things to work with. The picture shows you just what you need.

Make sure that the wire you have is covered. Such wire is called insulated wire. If you take off the insulation, or covering, you will find bright

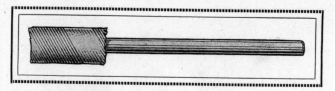

This wire is not insulated

copper wire inside. This is a picture of wire. The thick end part is insulated. The thin part has had the insulation taken off. Only the copper wire shows.

The insulation, or covering, on the wire is very important. The electricity flows along the copper wire. It cannot flow through the covering; so it keeps going right on along the wire.

Some things let electricity flow along them. They are called conductors. Copper is a very good conductor. Most metals are good conductors of electricity. That is, they let electricity flow along them.

The covering on the wire is usually made of cloth or rubber. These things do not conduct electricity. They do not let electricity flow along them. They are called nonconductors. Sometimes they are called insulators. Silk, glass, rubber, and cotton do not conduct electricity. They are all insulators, or nonconductors.

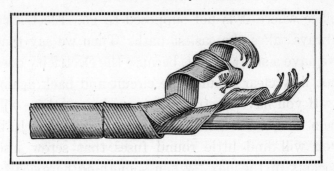

This is the way to insulate wire

When you wire your doorbell you want electricity to flow through the wire. If you did not insulate the wires leading to and from the bell the electricity might flow to some other place.

The electricity needs to flow from the dry cell to the bell, and then back again to the dry cell. It needs a clear path to flow along. This clear path is called a closed circuit.

When horses run a race they need a track to run on. They start at a certain spot and run around the track back to the starting place again.

Electricity has a path like that. It has to come back to the place where it started from. The path of electricity is called its circuit.

It sometimes happens that the insulation gets worn off the wire in places. The electric current may then leave the copper wire and jump to some

c

place where it is not supposed to go. Electricity always takes the easiest path. Then we say that we have a short circuit, because the electricity does not flow clear around the circuit and back again.

If you have electricity in your house, there will be a fuse box somewhere in your house, too. In it you will find little round fuses that screw into sockets in the box. When something happens to cause a short circuit along the wires, one or more of the fuses burns out, and the electric current is shut off. If the fuses did not blow out, the electric current might start a fire somewhere in your house.

Did your mother ever blow out a fuse when she was using the electric iron? Did you ever blow out a fuse when you were playing with your electric train? Whenever a fuse blows out there is probably a short circuit somewhere.

Here is the way to wire the bell.

First. Cut two pieces of insulated wire long enough to reach from the bell to the dry cell.

Second. Scrape the insulation off both ends of each wire. Be sure to scrape it all off.

Third. Polish the ends of the wire. Make them shine.

Fourth. Now fasten them as you see in the drawing on page 283. Pinch the wires tightly around the posts of the cell and the screws of the bell.

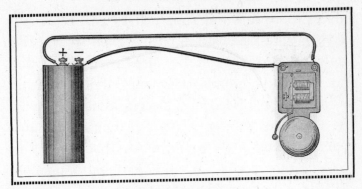

Would this bell ring?

If you have followed directions your bell will ring. It rings because the electricity has a closed circuit to flow through.

Do you want your bell to ring all the time? The cell would soon become weak if you let the bell ring all the time. The neighbors and your mother would probably object, too.

Of course when you want the bell to stop ringing all you have to do is unfasten one of the wires. It would then look like the drawing on page 284.

The circuit is not closed now. It is open. Electricity cannot flow through an open circuit; so the bell cannot ring.

Should you expect your guests to attach the wire every time they came to call? That wouldn't be polite, would it? You want the bell to be easy

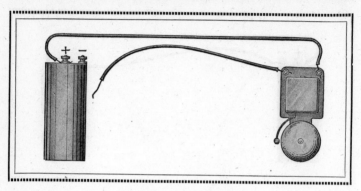

Would this bell ring?

for your guests to ring. So let's fasten a push button in the circuit. Do it as shown on the opposite page. Be sure to scrape the insulation off each end of the new piece of wire which you need.

Now your bell will ring only when the button is pressed.

Do you see the little piece of metal just below the button? When some one presses the button it pushes this piece of metal down so that it touches the wire to the bell. That closes the circuit. Electricity can flow from the cell to the button, then to the bell, and back to the cell. We say that we make a circuit for the electricity to pass through.

When you take your hand off the button you break the circuit. Now the metal does not touch

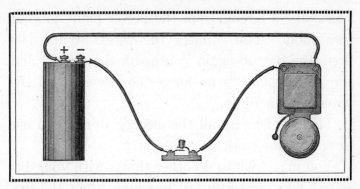

This is one way to wire a bell. Can you wire one of your own?

the wire to the bell. The electricity cannot get through because the circuit is broken.

Inside the bell itself there is a magnet. It was there when you bought the bell. When the current is turned on, the magnet pulls the clapper of the bell toward it. This breaks the circuit. The spring on the clapper pulls it back. This makes the circuit. The magnet pulls the clapper again. The spring jerks it back. In other words, the magnet and the spring make and break the circuit.

When you push the button you close the circuit, and the bell rings. Every time you take your hand off the button you break the circuit, and the bell stops ringing.

When you push the button on the wall of your room, your electric light goes on. That is because you make a circuit from the power plant to your own room. You connect the wires. When you press the button again you break the circuit, and the power plant is no longer connected with the wires in your room.

That is the way all the electric things you use in your home work.

You may wish to do other things with your dry cells. You may want to use more than the dry cell in wiring. There is only one thing to be careful about when using more than one cell.

Dry cells have two posts on top of them. These posts are the places where you connect the wires. The post in the center looks just like the post at the edge. But they are not alike.

The post in the center is the positive, or plus, post. The post on the outside is the negative, or minus, one. We use a plus sign (+) for the positive post. We use a minus sign (−) for the negative post. These posts are no more alike than addition and subtraction.

When you use two dry cells you may wire them as they are wired in the drawing at the top of page 287.

Do you see that the + post of one cell is wired to the − post of the other cell?

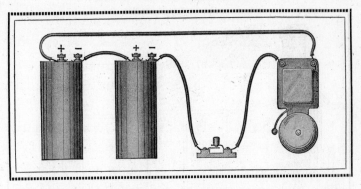

Sometimes you may wish to use more than one dry cell

3. How to Wire Lights

Do you want to know how to wire lights? You may have a small theater which needs lights.

Some smaller children may need to have their playhouse lighted. I know some children who helped some little folk in their school wire their playhouse.

One class of children made a large ship. They wanted lights on the masts of their ship. They wired it themselves.

You may want to know how to wire lights.

Be sure to scrape all the insulation off the ends of the wire. The two long pieces of wire are insulated. Wherever you put a socket for a light, you must scrape the insulation off at that place.

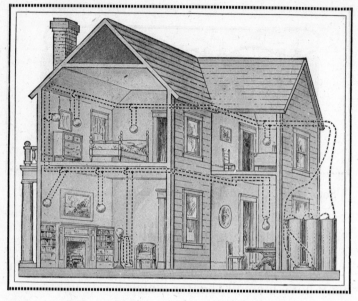

Some children wired this doll house for
lights. It may help you to learn how, too

That lets the electricity flow into the light
wires. Otherwise your lights would not work.

Do not let the two long wires touch each
other. If you do you will make a short circuit.

Your lights will stay on all the time unless
you use a push button. You know how to
connect that. Connect it just as you did for
the bell.

Here is one way to wire a playhouse. Notice
that the long wires do not cross each other.

Two pieces of wire have been spliced

4. How to Splice Wire

Sometimes you may need to fasten two pieces of wire together. This is called splicing the wire. This drawing will show you how to splice wire.

When the wires are fastened together, cover them with tape to insulate them.

5. How to Insulate Wires

You can insulate your own wires if you wish. Buy copper wire and electricians' tape. Wrap the tape around the wire. Be sure that none of the wire shows through. This tape is an insulator.

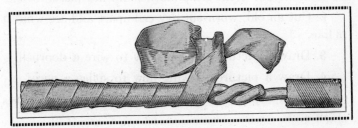

After two pieces of wire have been spliced
they must be covered with insulation tape

Things to Think About

1. Why are electric wires in a city often put beneath the streets?

2. What would you need in wiring a bell?

3. What is a conductor?

4. What is a closed circuit?

5. What causes a short circuit?

6. Electricity is now being used to keep people well. From a sun lamp our body can get the same kind of rays that we get from the sun. In winter, when it is difficult to get enough natural sun rays, these lamps are very valuable. They take the place of cod-liver oil, or bottled sunlight, as some people would say.

Things to Do

1. Make a list of all the electric things your mother has which your great-grandmother did not have.

2. Cut an old, worn-out dry cell apart and see what it is like.

3. Draw a picture showing how to wire a doorbell.

4. Draw a picture showing how to splice a wire.

5. Draw a picture showing how to wire a playhouse.

Problem 2 · Why Steam Has Power

1. The Work of Steam

All of you must have taken a ride on a train. Perhaps some of you have gone on long trips on trains. How fast you went! Fast trains go sixty or seventy miles an hour.

What made your train go? What power was there that made those big grinding wheels whiz down the track?

The power that made your train go so fast was probably steam. It may have been electricity.

Steam helps man in many ways. It drives large engines. It pulls heavy loads. It drives ships across the ocean. It furnishes power to the tiny tugboat that you have seen pulling such heavy loads behind it. It furnishes the power to run the steam shovels that dig the cellars for new buildings.

Let us see where steam gets its power and how it works.

Long, long ago people found out that steam had power. James Watt was one of the first men to put this power to work. He made it run an engine which pulled water up out of the coal mines in England. Although he did not make the very first steam engine, he did make the first one that would really work. Since that time many men have made and used steam engines.

2. Does Steam Have Power?

You all know what steam is. It is the gas which forms when water boils. You cannot see it, but it has power just the same.

Of course just heating water a little does not make steam. Do you remember that water changes to ice when the temperature goes below 32° F.? Water changes to steam when the temperature becomes 212° F. We call 212° F. the boiling point of water. We call 32° F. the freezing point of water. When water boils it changes to steam.

If you want to prove that steam has power ask your teacher to do this experiment. Do not do it without your teacher's help.

Put a little water into a test tube and hold it with a clamp.

The test tube will not break when heated. Other glass bottles can not be used, because they break when they are heated.

Hold the tube by the clamp over a flame.

The steam that formed in the tube blew the cork off

Let the water come to a boil. Take the tube from the flame, and cork the hole loosely with a rubber stopper. Be careful to have a cork which just fits. *Warning! Do not cork the tube tightly.*

Put the tube over the blaze again. Hold the corked end away from you. In a moment the cork will fly out of the neck of the tube.

Use your thermometer and test the water now. Is it 212° F.? It may not be just that. How near 212° F. is it?

You will wonder why the cork blew out of the tube.

When the water boiled it made steam. The steam needed more room than the water and air which were in the tube. It needed much more room.

One quart of water will make seventeen hundred quarts of steam. Think of it! The steam which the water made needed seventeen hundred times more room than the water itself. There was not so much room as that in the tube. So off went the cork.

Men now make steam in large metal boilers and use it to run many kinds of engines.

3. Cylinder and Piston Rod

Have you ever used an air pump to pump up your bicycle tires or your foot ball when they needed air? If you have, you will know what a cylinder and piston look like.

The bicycle pump looks like the drawing on the top of the next page.

The round part of the pump is a cylinder. In-

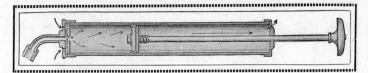

This is a cross section of a bicycle pump. Can
you find the cylinder, piston, and piston rod?

side the cylinder there is a rod with a disk at the
bottom. This rod is a piston rod. The disk at
the bottom is a piston. The piston fits closely
into the cylinder.

Steam engines have cylinders. The piston is
pushed back and forth in the cylinder by the
steam. There are two openings, or doors, in the
top of the cylinder to let steam out. You can see
them in the drawing on the next page.

When the piston rod is nearly to the end of
the cylinder, the door near it opens. This lets
steam in. The steam fills the space and tries to
get out. It pushes the piston down to the other
end of the cylinder to make more room for itself.

Now the door at the other end opens, and the
steam which enters there tries to get out, too. It
pushes the piston back again. The steam coming
in has so much force that it pushes the used steam,
on the other side of the piston, out through the
door again and into the exhaust pipe. This pipe

Looking into the cylinder of a steam engine.
Follow the direction of the arrows in each picture. Tell what happens to the piston in each

leads into the smokestack of the engine. Thus
the used steam escapes into the air and turns to
water again.

Back and forth goes the piston.

Another rod is fastened to the piston rod. It is

called a connecting rod because it connects the piston rod to the big driving wheel. As the steam works the piston in and out, it also works the rod and turns the wheel.

Now you know what makes the wheels go round.

Try to find the piston rod and cylinder at work on the next steam engine you see. Remember

1. Water is heated until it forms steam.
2. Steam needs more room than it has in the cylinder.
3. It pushes the piston back and forth in order to make more room.
4. The piston rod works the wheel.

 Things to Think About

1. Why does steam have power?

2. What useful things does steam do for us?

3. What things do we have now that run by steam which people who lived 250 years ago did not dream of having?

c

 *Things to Do*

1. Go to see a big steam locomotive. Try to find the boiler, piston rod, cylinder, and connecting rods.

2. Work the handle of a bicycle pump in and out and feel the air being pushed out of the rubber tube.

3. Draw a picture of a steam engine and label the different parts.

4. Read about George Stephenson and his work with the steam engine in "Historic Railroads," a book by Rupert Sargent Holland.

Science Words

This part of your book is really a science dictionary. It was made to help you find out the meanings of the science words which are used in your book. When you come across a new word in science and you wish to find out what that word means, look it up in this science dictionary. It is arranged alphabetically, just as your dictionary is.

After each word you will find a simple explanation of the meaning. If you use this science dictionary, you will be better able to understand what you read.

You will also find a number. This number tells you the first page in your book upon which each word was used. The Roman numerals after some of the words tell you whether the word has been used in Books I, II, or III of Pathways in Science.

Abdomen. The third part of an insect's body (p. 135)

Aërate. To mix with air. Water usually has some air in it (p. 80)

Air. A mixture of gases which we breathe. We live at the bottom of an ocean of air (p. 6; also in I, II, III)

Air pressure. Air is so light that it does not seem to weigh anything. Yet all the air above us does weigh something, and it presses down on us. This pressing is air pressure (p. 88; also in III)

Air-tight. Closed so tightly that air is shut out (p. 23)

Alcohol. A colorless liquid that looks like water (p. 272)

Antennæ. The feelers which insects have on their heads (p. 173)

Aphid. A small insect which sucks the juice of plants (p. 172)

Aquarium. A tank or bowl of water in which plants and animals may live (p. 73; also in I)

Arachnid. An animal which has eight legs and whose body is divided into two parts. A spider is an arachnid (p. 191)

Atmosphere. The part of the earth that is made up of gases. The air is the atmosphere (p. 10)

Bacteria. Very small plants. We need a microscope in order to study bacteria (p. 46)

Barometer. An instrument used to measure the air pressure (p. 87)

Beebread. Food made by bees for their young to eat after hatching (p. 139)

Beetle. A common kind of insect. A ladybug is a beetle (p. 199)

Boil. When we boil water, it turns into steam (p. 40; also in III)

Boll. The seed-holding part of the plant (p. 241)

Carbon dioxide. One of the gases found in the air (p. 106)

Caterpillar. Some insects look somewhat like worms for a time while they are growing up. At this time they are caterpillars (p. 186; also in II, III)

Cell. A small room made by bees for storing food and hatching the eggs (p. 143)

Circuit. A path for electricity (p. 281)

Clay. A very fine soil made from rocks. Clay is very sticky when wet (p. 259; also in II)

Cocoon. The silken cases in which certain insects rest while changing to become full-grown insects (p. 187; also in II, III)

Condense. When a gas like water vapor cools and changes to a liquid, it is said to condense. Clouds are condensed water vapor (p. 75)

Conductor. Anything through which electricity will flow. Copper is a good conductor of electricity (p. 280)

Cone. The part of a volcano from which smoke, gas, ashes, and melted rock come. The volcano builds its own cone out of ashes and the rock which has melted and then hardened (p. 98)

Connecting rod. A rod which connects the piston rod to the driving wheel (p. 297)

Core. The inside of the earth. An apple has a core (p. 96)

Cultivate. To stir and break up the top of the soil (p. 264)

Cylinder. A long hollow tube. Pumps have cylinders (p. 294)

Decay. Rot. Trees decay after they have fallen (p. 260)

Dense. Thick (p. 30)

Dependent. Animals are dependent upon plants because they get their food from plants (p. 253)

Dissolve. When a solid becomes part of a liquid it is said to dissolve. Sugar dissolves in water (p. 15; also in III)

Dormant. Very quiet (p. 96)

Drone. One of the kinds of honeybee in a beehive (p. 133)

Dry cell. Dry cells furnish electricity. They are sometimes used to ring door bells and run electric motors (p. 277)

Dye. A color. Clothes can be dyed (p. 246; also in III)

Earth. The big ball or world on which we live (p. 5; also in I, III)

Earthquake. The shaking of the surface of the earth (p. 99)

Electric current. When electricity flows it is called an electric current (p. 281)

Electrician. A person who works upon anything electrical (p. 289)

Erosion. The carrying away of soil or rock by wind or water (p. 69)

Erupt. To throw out. A geyser erupts water and sometimes steam (p. 96)

Evaporate. To change from a liquid to a gas (p. 72; also in I, III)

Exhaust pipe. A pipe which carries away steam or gas which has been used in the cylinder (p. 295)

Expand. To spread out or become larger (p. 46)

Fahrenheit. Most of our thermometers use the Fahrenheit scale. On this scale water freezes at 32° and boils at 212° (p. 39)

Female. A mother animal is a female animal (p. 153)

Fertilize. Farmers fertilize the soil when they use manure or other materials to make the soil better for growing plants (p. 262)

Fertilizer. Something put on the soil to help plants grow (p. 261)

Fogs. Water vapor which has condensed in the air, close to the earth. Fogs are clouds near the ground (p. 34; also in II)

Fungus (*plural*, **fungi**). Certain plants, such as toadstools, mushrooms, and puffballs, are fungi (p. 268)

Fuse. Fuses melt or burn out whenever there is a short circuit. Fuses help to keep electricity from starting fires (p. 282)

Gas. A gas is like air. It fills all the space it can (p. 6; also in III)

Gaseous. Like gas (p. 6)

Geyser. An opening in the earth's surface through which steam and water are often pushed into the air (p. 25)

Gills. Parts of the body which fish use for breathing. Gills are somewhat like our lungs (p. 210; also in I, III)

Glacier. Snow and ice which has collected on high mountains. It slowly moves down the mountain as more snow piles on it (p. 83)

Gravel. A very coarse soil made from rocks (p. 259)

Gravitation. The sun, moon, and stars have a force called gravitation (p. 10)

Gravity. A force which pulls things to the earth (p. 9)

Herb. A kind of plant. Plants which do not have stems of wood like trees are called herbs (p. 244)

Hurricane. A very strong wind (p. 85)

Hydroplane. An airplane which flies into the air from water and returns to the water (p. 6)

Ice Age. A time in the history of the earth when the climate was so cold that ice and snow hundreds of feet deep covered many parts of Europe, Canada, and the United States for many years (p. 84)

Iceberg. Part of a glacier which has broken off and floats in the ocean (p. 84)

Insect. An animal which has six legs and whose body is divided into three parts (p. 129; also in I, II, III)

Insulation. A covering to an electric wire which prevents electricity from flowing anywhere except along the wire (p. 279)

Insulators. See Nonconductors (p. 280)

Invisible. Cannot be seen (p. 41)

Larva (*plural*, **larvæ**). When insects are larvæ they look somewhat like worms. Some are called caterpillars at this time (p. 145)

Lava. Melted rock from a volcano (p. 96)

Lime. A white substance somewhat like earth. Lime is used with sand in the making of mortar and plaster (p. 261)

Liquid. Water and oil are liquids. Liquids can be carried about in pails (p. 6)

Loam. A mixture of fine soil and parts of decayed plants (p. 259)

Magnet. A piece of iron which can pull to it other pieces of iron and steel (p. 285; also in I, III)

Magnifying glass. A glass which makes objects look larger than they are. A reading glass is a magnifying glass (p. 166; also in I)

Male. A father animal is a male animal (p. 153)

Mammals. Warm-blooded animals whose young are fed on their mothers' milk. Mice and elephants are mammals (p. 209)

Manure. A kind of fertilizer (p. 261)

Microscope. Several magnifying glasses held together so that very small objects may be studied (p. 152)

Migrate. Certain animals migrate, or travel from one place to another, at a certain time every year (p. 222)

Mineral. Something which is not animal or vegetable. Rocks are made up of minerals (p. 101)

Mold. A kind of plant which starts from spores. Mold is sometimes found on bread (p. 269)

Molten. Melted, become a liquid (p. 26)

Mulch. Loose, fine soil (p. 265)

Nectar. A sweet liquid found in flowers. Bees use nectar in making honey (p. 137; also in I)

Nitrogen. One of the gases found in the air (p. 108)

Nonconductor. Glass is a nonconductor, because it does not carry electricity (p. 280)

Oxygen. One of the gases found in the air (p. 19)

Pest. A plant or animal which causes trouble is called a pest (p. 180)

Piston. A tight-fitting piece which slides back and forth in a cylinder. All automobiles have cylinders and pistons (p. 294)

Piston rod. The long rod fastened to the piston and moving back and forth with it (p. 294)

Pollen. A dust found inside flowers (p. 139; also in I)

Pollen baskets. The baskets on the hind legs of the worker bees, in which they carry pollen (p. 139)

Pores. Very small openings in the leaves of plants or the skin of animals. We have pores in our skin (p. 75)

Purify. To clean (p. 29)

Queen bee. A mother bee (p. 135)

Reservoir. A lake, usually made by man, for storing water (p. 78)

Resin. Sticky material from pine trees (p. 157)

Revolve. To turn around another object. The earth revolves around the sun once a year (p. 55)

Rigid. Very steady and firm (p. 26)

Rotating. Turning around as a spinning top. The earth rotates once a day (p. 52)

Sac. A bag used by the bee to hold the sweet liquid it takes from flowers (p. 139)

Sand. A coarse soil made from rocks (p. 259; also in I, II)

Science. When we study about why things happen and how they happen, we are studying science (p. 165)

Scientists. Those people who study carefully to learn "how" and "why" about many things (p. 9; also in III)

Silt. A fine soil made from rocks (p. 259)

Social. Some animals are called social because many of them will live together. Honeybees are social animals (p. 125)

Solid. Anything which holds its shape (p. 37)

Solitary. Being alone. A solitary animal is one which lives most of its life alone (p. 124)

Spinnerets. The spinning parts of a spider's body (p. 192)

Spore. A very small part of some plants, which can start a new plant (p. 268)

Stalactite. A stone built in the ceiling of some caves by the work of running water. Each drop of water carries a small bit of mineral, and after thousands of years the small bits make a rock which looks like an icicle (p. 76)

Stalagmite. A stone built on the floor of some caves by the work of running water. Stalagmites are shaped like stalactites or icicles, but they are made "up-side-down" (p. 76)

Steam. A gas that cannot be seen which is made when water boils (p. 40)

Termite. One kind of social insect. Termites have homes like ants, but their homes are much larger (p. 178)

Thermometer. An instrument used to tell temperature (p. 39; also in I, II)

Thorax. That part of an insect's body to which the six legs and four wings are fastened (p. 135)

Tornadoes. A whirling wind (p. 85)

Ventilate. We ventilate home and school in order that the air may make us feel comfortable and help us keep well (p. 20)

Ventilator. Any opening used to ventilate a room (p. 116)

Volcano. A mountain which can erupt melted rock and gases (p. 25)

Water vapor. When water evaporates, it goes into the air and becomes water vapor (p. 63)

Worker bees. The bees that do all the work in the bee-hive except laying the eggs (p. 136)

Index

What This Index Is

This Index is a guide and has been placed in this book to help you. It is made in alphabetical order just as your dictionary is. In fact, if you know how to use your dictionary, you will also know how to use this Index.

"The Earth and Living Things" answers many questions about the earth, and plants and animals living upon it. Many times you will be in a hurry to find the answer to a certain question. Of course, if you want to find the answer quickly, this Index is just the place to look for help.

How To Use This Index

A guide is of little value to you unless you really know how to use it. Suppose that you learn how to use this Index guide right now.

You may wish to know what *icebergs* are. Look for the word *iceberg* in the Index. Remember that the words in this Index are all listed alphabetically. That is, all the words beginning with *a* come first; the words beginning with *b* follow; then those beginning with *c* and so on. Look in the *i* words for *iceberg*. It looks like this:

Icebergs, 84

The 84 means page 84. Turn to that page and you will find out about icebergs there.

Sometimes the book gives information about a certain question on more than one page. Let's find out what to do in a case like that. Suppose that you want to find out about the carpenter ant. Look for the word *ants* in your Index. *Ants* begins with *a*. Where will you look for it in the Index? *Ants* is called the "key" word. After it you will find several "helping," or descriptive, words. Here they are:

Ants, 165; black, 167; the
classes of, 168; red, 175;
farmer, 177; carpenter,
178; white, 178

In this case there is so much information in the book about ants that the "helping" words are put in the Index so that you can find what you want quickly. You want to know about the carpenter ant. Read the "helping" words. Do you find what you are looking for? The number following the word *carpenter* means the number of the page on which you will find a story about the carpenter ant.

Using the Index comes to be fun. It will save you much time. Practice finding words in it. Soon you will be able to find the material you want quickly. Most of your other books have indexes. They are used in the same way.

The Index

c